Larry –

Here's to Hopefully working on a few "Harvest" together!

MW00880503

HARVEST

THE DEFINITIVE GUIDE
TO SELLING YOUR COMPANY

DAVID C. TOLSON & CHRISTOPHER J. YOUNGER

Managing Directors for CapitalValue Advisors, LLC

Outskirts Press, Inc.
Denver, Colorado

TABLE OF CONTENTS

FOREWORD AND ACKNOWLEDGEMENTS

According to the U.S. Small Business Administration, there are an estimated six million businesses in the United States with fewer than five hundred employees, 60% of which are owned by men or women over the age of 45. Over the next 10-20 years, most of these businesses will either transition to owners' children, shut down, or be sold. The smartest owners will consider and plan for these transitions years before they retire or exit their businesses. Unfortunately, many business owners are so focused on the day-to-day operations of their companies that they give little attention to an exit strategy for when they want to retire or transition out of their business. For the minority of business owners who do plan for the future of their business without them, many struggle to understand what their business is truly worth, both to themselves and in the broader market. Moreover, they are likely to be mystified by the whole process of selling a company, having heard horror stories from their friends and colleagues who may have endured a difficult sale of their business...or worse, a failed attempt at a sale.

We run our own boutique investment bank as well as a private equity firm, so we enjoy the opportunity to interact with middle-market businesses and business owners on a daily basis. Entrepreneurs are a special breed – they are passionate, committed, enthusiastic, optimistic, and fun to be around. They are calculated risk-takers, and they bring a lot of value to their communities. We are privileged to have had the opportunity to help clients transition their businesses to new owners who will hopefully be just as passionate about our clients' customers and employees as well as the reputation of their businesses in the community. Having managed dozens of sale transactions, we wanted to share some of this experience with other business owners who may be considering an eventual exit of their business. This book is designed to help business owners understand different valuation methods, and in it we pose a series of questions to help you assess whether you are ready to sell. We also provide a detailed analysis of what actually happens when a company is brought to market and ultimately sold. In short, we want to arm you with all the information you need when you are considering the sale of your company.

Over our collective history, we have completed more than fifty transactions as buyer, seller, or advisor. From our varied experiences in business management, transactions, valuation, and operations, we have broad expertise with the unique requirements of business transactions. In addition, we have years of direct operating experience with companies of all sizes, from managing start-ups to leading a billion-dollar communications company. We think this varied experience gives us a unique and practical perspective on the business of mergers and acquisitions.

Unlike a lot of transaction advisors, we have managed businesses before and after a sale, so we are particularly sensitive to the operating issues business owners face during the entire life cycle of a sale transaction. We hope this perspective will be helpful and assist you in building value in your business, whether you decide to sell, buy, or hold. Our goal with this book is to convince you that the time you spend today thinking about the ultimate sale or transition of your business will yield some of the greatest rewards you will ever experience related to your business, both financially and personally.

A book like ours is only as good as the experience of its authors. We have had the benefit of conducting transactions with dozens of great business owners. From these transactions and our interactions with business owners, bankers, lawyers, accountants, and others, we have learned the lessons which form the basis for this book's content. Although too numerous to list, we want to acknowledge their contributions to our learning, education, and experience.

We also want to recognize the contributions of our employees at

CapitalValue, Roy Patterson and Zack Gibson, and Chris's wife, Maribeth, who endured several reviews and offered insightful comments and help. All of the mistakes and errors are of course ours.

Finally, from our lawyers we want to remind you that this book is no substitute for proper legal, tax, accounting, and transaction advice. Our review of the acquisition process in this book is by necessity a broad treatment of the business of transactions, and in no way should be relied on when planning or consummating your own transaction. As we reiterate throughout our book, you should retain the best professional advice you can to ensure your transaction goes smoothly and with the fewest number of issues and challenges. Our goal with this book is simply to help you and your advisors spot potential problems and plan accordingly.

Our best wishes to you for a bountiful Harvest.

Addendum: March 31, 2009

As we go to print with *HARVEST*, we are experiencing perhaps the worst economy and market correction since the Great Depression. Public equity markets worldwide are down over 50 percent in many regions, and credit flow has slowed to a crawl. Many company owners are experiencing the worst general business conditions they have seen in their lifetimes, and are rightly concerned about the future. All of this, of course, has an impact on the market for private businesses. With less freely available credit and deteriorating business conditions, valuations for private companies have come down, and transactions are more challenging to complete. However, what we have found historically and are finding even today is that there is always a market for good businesses run by honest, ethical, hard-working, and talented managers. While valuations may take a long time to recover to the lofty heights we experienced in the past decade, what we see today are reasonable valuations with more responsible capital structures utilizing less debt, all of which we believe is positive for the market overall.

Recessions are an important and recurring part of any free market economy and are designed to work out excesses and inefficiencies in the market. In good and bad times, the best businesses develop new strategies for keeping costs low and customer value high, and in many cases emerge with an even stronger market position after a recession.

The lessons of this book are equally applicable in good or challenging markets. Indeed, the need to run a well-organized, strategically sound business is even more important in a tough market than in a market where every company has an opportunity to sell. As a business owner, use these challenging times to re-examine your business and stretch your capabilities to put further distance between you and your competitors. We hope our book can help you ask the right questions and develop these strategies.

-- *David and Chris*

CHAPTER 1
PREPARING TO HARVEST – ARE YOU READY FOR THIS?

M any business owners dream about the day they will sell their business – a big check, a little rest and relaxation, an opportunity to pursue hobbies, or time to think about a new venture or project long ignored while they had the obligations of running a business. In our experience, however, as the closing date looms a sense of panic can set in for a business owner. An owner will ask questions like: Did I sell at the wrong time? Am I getting a fair deal? Am I getting enough out of the deal to truly retire or start my next venture? Isn't my business worth more than this? What am I going to do after the sale?

This book is designed to help you think systematically about each of the steps involved in harvesting value through the sale of your business – evaluating your financial and other needs, planning your exit objectives, valuing your business, understanding financial statements and legal agreements, finding a pool of potential buyers, enhancing the value of your business through proper positioning, timing and operational improvement, negotiating the transaction, and closing the deal. The first step we recommend for any company owner contemplating the sale of his company is to enlist a team of trusted advisors who have transactional experience and can help the business owner think through the myriad issues ahead of time and plan for the inevitable challenges that will arise. The advisory team should include an attorney, accountant, financial advisor, and investment banker or transaction advisor, and ideally should be in place well in advance of an actual transaction. It is important that these advisors have or can develop a deep understanding of your business and your personal needs. It is also crucial that your professional advisors have transaction experience. The level of transaction experience is particularly important when considering your attorney and investment banker, as their skills, experience, and judgment will be critical to managing the deal through the pitfalls that invariably plague transactions. We tell our clients that deals will die at least three "deaths" before they close – transactions are often charged with emotion, and as a result, can run off the rails on occasion. Having an experienced advisor will help cooler heads prevail and will ensure you have someone who has the creativity and experience to navigate the minefields.

When contemplating the sale of their company, some business owners will have dozens of questions and reservations, so it is no wonder some business owners get cold feet at the closing table. And yet we have seen others who are completely at peace and excited about life after closing. What is the difference between these two types of owners, and how do you ensure you are confident about your decision to sell? To answer these questions and understand this dynamic better, you need to first understand why a business owner actually goes to the trouble of trying to sell his business.

<u>Exit Objectives: Why Do Business Owners Sell?</u> Running a business is hard work. The initial thrill of starting a new venture or acquiring a company is quickly replaced with the stresses of employees, customers, making payroll, and being the first one in the door and the last one to lock up at night. For some business owners, this can get tiresome, leading them to think life must be better without the constant stress accompanying the role of an owner. Sometimes this is a fleeting thought, while at other times, particularly when times get tough, these anxieties can become an obsession.

We have met hundreds of business owners who fall into this category: Tired. They are tired of the daily grind, tired from all the stress, tired of the industry, and tired of dealing with employees and customers. Unfortunately, this is precisely the *wrong* time to be thinking about selling. Your business is like any other asset – if not properly presented, positioned, and cared for, it won't return the maximum value to you, the owner of this asset, whether you are seventy and looking to retire or you are thirty and planning to begin your next venture.

When a business owner is tired, more often than not it is because his business has reached a plateau, is not doing particularly well, or is suffering from a lack of attention, all of which typically result in lackluster business performance, or worse. A savvy buyer will immediately see whether the business is in "steady state" or deteriorating, or whether the business is growing and has an opportunity for continued growth. In most cases, buyers will pay more for a growing business than for a "steady state" or declining business. We have learned through dozens of transactions that in most growing and profitable businesses, the value of the business continues to increase through the sale process which enhances both a seller's negotiating position and the likelihood of a deal actually closing. In a no-growth or deteriorating business, its value will decline over time, which means buyers are more prone to get cold feet or question the original deal they proposed, which only prolongs the transaction process and increases the odds for a busted deal. As a result, tired sellers make for unsatisfying transactions.

On the other hand, business owners who are enthusiastic about their business and its potential, but want to consider their exit options, are much more likely to secure a transaction that meets or exceeds their needs and expectations. When a business is growing and has solid prospects for continued revenue and profit growth, it will command a premium valuation in the market. A seller's excitement, enthusiasm, and optimism are all contagious to potential buyers. Buyers will in turn build on the seller's enthusiasm with their own ideas and plans, which should result in a higher valuation and a deal that is more likely to close. Sometimes an owner of a growing business can feel like he left money on the table after a sale, but in our experience growing businesses sell faster, at higher valuations, and with more predictability than shrinking or stagnating businesses. When we engage clients early, we advise them to "sell on the way up," as it is hard to predict when the "top" will be reached, and selling "on the way down" is a tougher proposition.

Pay Attention to Subtle Messages. As we discussed, sophisticated buyers look at a seller's motivation for selling as a proxy for how they as a buyer should feel about the business. For example, a poten-

3

tial buyer once asked a client of ours how involved he wanted to stay in the business after closing. Our client responded, "If the right buyer could come with a big bucket of cash, I'd prefer to ride off into the sunset and be done." As you might expect, his attempt at lighthearted humor fell flat.

Our client actually did not really feel this way – he was genuinely concerned about his customers, employees, and the future reputation of his business. However, buyers pay attention to these subtle comments or jokes, and they definitely color the way buyers feel about the business. Conversely, when sellers express their hopes and dreams about their business following acquisition, a buyer can then build on and develop his own vision of success with the company, guided by the seller's enthusiasm. An ideal seller is one who is leaving the business for legitimate reasons (e.g., retirement, going into a different business, a serial entrepreneur, etc.), but who takes time to thoroughly and thoughtfully test each buyer's interest in taking care of his company's employees, customers, and other stakeholders.

A seller should interview a potential buyer just as vigorously and intensely as the buyer would interview a seller. This communicates to the buyer that the business owner cares as much about the future of his business as he does about the check at closing. This strategy gives a seller more information about a buyer's motivations and expertise (which can be important in negotiations as we will discuss later), and it creates in the buyer a sense of having to prove himself "worthy" of consideration by the seller, tilting the negotiating tables slightly to the seller's advantage.

Fix the Business First. On occasion, a seller's business may be in such trouble that the seller is overwhelmed and feels he has no viable alternatives to either selling the company at a fire-sale price or shutting it down. This is obviously a terrible position for a seller, and it is why we advise business owners whenever possible to fix the business issues they face first, and only then think about selling. This may sound obvious, but you would be surprised how many potential sellers believe selling their business is the only alternative for solving their problems. Most sellers have spent the better part of their lifetimes working in and on their businesses, and it is tragic when an owner sells his business for less than it is worth simply because he is not able to resolve underlying operating issues. In our experience, many buyers can't see past a company's flaws or are unwilling to undertake the uncertainty of a turnaround (at least at a price acceptable to a seller). In these circumstances, an outside consultant can sometimes help, either by giving a business owner a fresh, objective perspective or a friendly ear, or by providing guidance to help resolve the underlying issues.

Yet whether an owner ends up selling his business or keeping it, working to improve the underlying condition of the business is almost always the best strategy unless the owner does not have and cannot find enough capital to sustain the business long enough to fix it. By focusing on underlying operating issues, a seller can often resolve some of the underlying pressure to sell the company, which increases the value of the business to the owner regardless of whether or not a sale occurs. It is hard work, we know, and some business owners may be so tired and frustrated that a sale seems like the best option, but selling a troubled business with a disenchanted owner has very slim odds for success.

<u>Post-Sale Planning – A Requirement</u>. One of the first questions we ask potential clients is what they plan to do after the sale. For us, this is a good way to determine whether the owner has thoroughly considered the implications of a sale. As we highlighted above, some business owners are simply tired and want to sell under the assumption that selling their business has to be better than continuing to operate it. Too often, though, these business owners find that life after a sale, particularly a sale at below-market value, is not necessarily better, and may mean they have to go back to work. Business owners should have a clear picture, preferably a written plan, of what they will do following a sale and carefully compare that plan to the prospect of continuing to own the company. This written plan can be as detailed or as generic as the business owner desires, but it should include specific activities, particularly for the first 30 days or so, as this period of time can be the most challenging. This game plan can include goals, objectives, and/or major activities (travel, for example)

for the year following closing. Most business owners and entrepreneurs are active people – by nature they are builders. When the time comes for them to stop building, they can become highly disillusioned and dissatisfied. Having sold businesses ourselves, the several months following a sale can be pretty unsettling as you rebuild your daily routine, take care of matters that have been ignored, and generally adjust.

Life after a sale does not have to be difficult – we know of many entrepreneurs who have gone on to start new businesses, pursue charity work, get absorbed in hobbies, or who have simply adapted well to retirement. However, if a business owner has not thoughtfully considered each of these options, it is possible that a sale will be unfulfilling. Until the closing date, a business owner goes to the office every day, has employees who take direction (or not!), and is generally "in control." After the closing date, a business owner may become an employee of or consultant to the new owner, or even retire.

In any of these situations life is different, and a business owner needs to contemplate this new life and how to adjust to it. Just as a good business strategy requires solid planning, life after a sale also requires careful consideration. Having a plan in which you lay out in detail what you want to do and accomplish helps you adjust to your new life more easily and with more confidence. Our deal experience is full of examples of sellers getting "cold feet" at the closing table: they question their real desire to complete the transaction, even though the decision to sell may be in their best interests and the terms of the sale might be the deal of a lifetime. For business owners who have worked through a personal post-closing planning process, the actual closing can be a great turning point as they embark on the next chapter of their lives.

Financial Needs Post-Closing. Too often, business owners have only a vague notion of their true financial needs, making the decision to sell anxiety-ridden and problematic. One of the questions a seller should answer before considering a sale is how a sale will or will not meet his financial needs going forward. While owning their business, business owners can earn significant income and as a result, some business owners enjoy many of life's luxuries (with its attendant costs). Some business owners diligently save and wisely diversify their holdings, but for the majority of business owners, much, if not most, of their net worth is locked up in the equity value of their company. In any case, prior to making the decision to sell, a potential seller should carefully evaluate his or her required living standards and other financial needs, preferably with a professional financial planner.

In our practice, we will rarely take a business to market until we have completed a detailed valuation and the seller has compared this valuation to the analysis prepared by his financial planner. In addition to the qualitative reasons sellers might get cold feet, a seller who does not understand, or who over- or underestimates his financial needs, is likely to have significant reservations about selling his business as closing day approaches because he will be uncertain about his financial future after a sale. If a seller has thoroughly prepared a financial needs analysis with his financial planner, then the decision to sell can be made with confidence that his monetary needs after a sale will be satisfied.

The analysis of a seller's financial "needs" is highly subjective and in our experience benefits greatly from the advice of a financial planner who is trained to ask the right questions and prepare models based on different market, economic, personal, and other factors. Through this analysis, a seller is able to really understand what is required in cash at closing so that he is able to make informed, well-reasoned decisions about the sale of his business.

In reviewing your financial needs, be prepared to discuss your monthly "burn rate," or the cash you require each month just to live (this can include mortgage payments/rent, car payments, food, clothing, insurance, education, medical expenses, and utilities). Then consider your desired level of discretionary spending (vacations, toys, or other items that are "nice to have" but not necessary). You may also have other needs, including alimony, care for parents or children, upcoming college expenses, and other expenses you will need to consider.

7

Finally, you should compare this list of expenses with the expenses you expect to incur post-closing. An individual's expenses following a closing can vary greatly depending on the individual (e.g., no more need to wear suits to work or incur commuting costs, but your vacation plans might get a little more exotic). Once you have evaluated the magnitude and timing of these expenses, you will be able to intelligently determine what your financial needs truly are and what your discretionary spending assumptions do to your ultimate financial requirements. If you are armed with this information, the decision to sell and on what terms is much less stressful.

In short, preparing to sell a business is no different from any other business process. To be successful, you need to know what your ultimate objectives are and why, and then map out the steps required to accomplish your objectives. You may have heard the phrase, "Activity without a plan can often be mistaken for progress." In the case of managing what is likely your most valuable asset, you cannot afford to be without a well-considered plan. The first step in that plan is developing a detailed understanding of what you really need to accomplish with the sale of your business. The next step is to gain a much deeper understanding for what your company is worth in the broader market, and what factors can drive value up or down. Let's now look at business valuation.

CHAPTER 2

Once you have a handle on your financial and other requirements from a sale, you will need to understand what your business is worth and how its value relates to your stated needs and exit objectives. This chapter will help you learn how to value a business – from the perspective of a seller, a buyer, and as an objective observer. Most sellers value their business more highly than average buyers, for a variety of reasons. Conversely, different types of buyers value businesses differently based on their own needs and assumptions about future performance. Objective observers, or what we commonly refer to as "market participants," will tend to look at valuation from a number of different perspectives, but will conclude their valuation based primarily on expected future cash flows. However, whether you are a buyer or a seller or you simply want to understand valuation better, you need to start with the most objective set of facts you can put together and work from there.

Too often we see both buyers and sellers get derailed because of fairly predictable emotional responses, which is why it is important for you as a company owner to use your advisors and be willing to listen to objective feedback and input, both negative and positive. As a seller, your decision to sell will obviously depend on your own specific business and personal needs, and must be weighed against continuing to operate your business as your next best alternative. This chapter aims to help you understand valuation better so that you can think more objectively about your business and about your decision to sell or continue operating.

When we are advising owners on mergers and acquisitions, our clients always begin by asking us what their business is worth. As with most assets that do not enjoy a high degree of liquidity (in contrast to stock in a public company, for example), the value of a privately-held business can and does vary significantly based on the perspective of the person doing the valuation. While we primarily value our clients' businesses based on widely accepted, quantitative valuation methodologies that attempt to capture the "market" value of a company, one of the things we encourage business owners to consider is the worth of the business to them personally (both quantitatively and qualitatively).

In many circumstances, an owner's expectation and assessment of the value of his or her business will be very different from what a standard market valuation would provide. Most financial and strategic buyers will use similar methods to value businesses, which is why it is critically important for you to understand how these methodologies work. However, keep in mind that even when using similar methodologies, buyers can reach different valuations based on different perceptions of industry, market, and company risk as well as different rationales for completing an acquisition.

Standard Valuation Methodologies. Consider first the three approaches for performing an objective valuation of a business: the asset approach, the market approach, and the income approach. The *market approach* is based on data from similar transactions in the private market to determine approximate market value. The *asset approach* is simply the net asset value of a company based on an assessment of a company's tangible and intangible assets less its liabilities – this is useful to establish a baseline value for a business. The *income approach* (sometimes referred to as the *discounted cash flow* or *capitalization of earnings approach)*, is probably the most widely used methodology, and attempts to estimate the future free cash flow a company will generate, and uses an appropriate discount rate to calculate the present value of these future cash flows.

A solid valuation will consider each of these three methodologies and determine an overall assessment of fair market value. Ultimately, valuation is an assessment of the present value of estimated future free cash flow in the context of market, industry, and specific company risk – the higher the perceived level of risk in an investment, the lower the resulting valuation. We will explore this in more detail below.

Business Owner Valuation. Notice that none of these approaches considers the subjective value of a company to the business owner, which in many cases will be higher than fair market value. Why is this? One reason may be that business owners are not adequately informed about market valuation (or they may be overly optimistic about how their business compares to other businesses in the industry). Alternatively, a business owner may receive real benefits from owning a business that a potential purchaser either may not find value in, or is not willing to pay additional consideration for in a transaction.

Because valuation is ultimately an assessment of risk, the most likely reason an owner will value his business more highly than the market is that he understands his business and its risks at a much deeper level than anyone else, and will often ascribe less risk to the operation of his business than a less informed buyer. For example, in our private equity firm we once looked at an acquisition of a construction contractor who had almost a year's worth of backlog on the books, which represented a whopping 70% growth in revenues over the prior year. The owner of course wanted to value the business based on the expected earnings represented by his backlog, but because we could never get as comfortable as he was about the underlying contracts, costs, and margin assumptions, our valuation for his business was substantially below his. This difference in perceived risk finds its way into almost all discussions about the future, and not being intimately familiar with the target company's industry or market simply increases the level of perceived risk for any rational buyer, which will result in a lower valuation.

In addition to differences in perceived risk, business owners also enjoy benefits that extend beyond simply capturing the earnings of a company. Let's take the hypothetical example of WidgetCo and its owner, Steve Smith. Last year, WidgetCo generated $10 million in annual sales and had pre-tax income of $1 million. Mr. Smith takes a salary of $200,000, enjoys health insurance at a lower cost than can

11

be obtained privately (if at all, for that matter), and has the benefit of other "perks" (company car, business trips that double as vacation time for him and his wife, and other perfectly legal fringe benefits). In the typical acquisition environment, a buyer will usually give a seller the benefit of "adding back" (or adjusting) some of these costs in determining the estimated future cash flow of the business (assuming these are costs a buyer would not expect to incur going forward). However, savvy buyers understand that some of these costs are hard to completely eliminate, and will apply some sort of "haircut" to these proposed adjustments to earnings.

For example, Mr. Smith's salary of $200,000 may be over, under, or at market rates for general managers of similar businesses – the new buyer will need to hire a manager, so the difference between the new manager's cost and the departing owner's salary is typically all a buyer will allow as an adjustment to earnings. As a result, although Mr. Smith is receiving the benefit of collecting his salary today while he owns the business, he is unlikely to reap much, if any, reward from his salary upon the sale of the business in the form of a higher purchase price. Put another way, if Mr. Smith is no longer working, he can no longer reasonably expect to receive the benefit of a market-based salary for his work (although we consistently see sellers attempting to add back all of their compensation to arrive at an adjusted earnings number).

In assessing the value of his business, Mr. Smith, like most business owners, will attach some non-financial value to owning his business, which is very hard to assign a market value. For example, Mr. Smith, having built his business from start-up to a very profitable $10 million business, has relied on key employees to whom he may have an attachment or loyalty. He has cultivated long-term relationships with key customers and suppliers who have helped him build his business, and he will likely enjoy some standing in his community as a business leader as a result of owning a successful business. If he is like most business owners, he will be concerned about the well-being of each of these constituencies, which again makes owning the business in some ways more valuable to him than selling the business. Each of these benefits is very hard to quantify, and there are very few business buyers who would be willing to pay for such value, yet these benefits are very real for the Mr. Smiths of the world.

Another reason business owners may attach non-financial value to owning their business is that most successful business owners are successful because they have invested years of diligent, concerted effort into building their business. Many business owners are "Type A" personalities and are passionate about their business, their employees, and their customers. Indeed, these are likely to be some of the primary reasons why they have been successful. Although many business owners will complain about the hours and stress of owning a business, we have seen several examples in which business owners who have sold their business experience a period of confusion, depression, or simple frustration at not being "in the game" anymore. They are lost without challenging work to do on a daily basis. This is not true for all business owners, of course, and some business owners adapt very well to life off the payroll, but the value a business owner might attach to having these types of day-to-day challenges and corresponding gratification and fulfillment will almost certainly not be appreciated by a potential buyer from a financial perspective.

Alternative Investments. In addition to the non-financial benefits a business owner is likely to attach to his business, a business owner also needs to understand the different types of returns he is likely to generate with alternative investments. For example, assume Mr. Smith is able to sell the stock in his business for $5 million, and after taxes keeps $4 million. In today's stock market, he would be very fortunate indeed to generate a 10% pre-tax return on his investments, or $400,000. This pales in comparison with the $1.2 million in earnings he received while he owned his business (his salary plus his company's pre-tax profits). As a result, Mr. Smith may demand more up front for his business to compensate for the less attractive returns he will generate in the broader market. Of course, his risk is likely much lower in owning a diversified basket of publicly traded stocks and bonds, but if he operates a quality business, he can somewhat mitigate the impact of the higher risk in owning a single business.

13

As suggested above, in many instances a business owner will attach a higher value to his or her business than the market or standard valuation methodology would dictate. It is important to understand why this occurs so that you as a potential buyer or seller can either creatively resolve these differences in valuation, or quickly move on if your valuation is dramatically different from a potential buyer's valuation. In addition, it is important for any owner of a business to have carefully considered his financial and personal objectives to ensure that a sale of his business will meet or exceed these objectives. A personal financial planner can help in this regard, which we recommend to all of our clients prior to actively marketing their business. The worst outcome for a business owner selling his business is to find after a year or two that he must go back to work in order to meet his financial objectives.

Given that your business is likely worth more to you than others, how exactly do you go about determining what your company is worth in the broader market? To make sure you have your bases covered, a solid business valuation will consider all valuation approaches: market, asset, and income (discounted cash flow/ capitalization of earnings).

Market Approach. In many cases, the market approach is the most accurate way to get a handle on what your business would be worth because it is based on how buyers in the market currently value comparable companies based on actual transactions. Similar to publicly traded companies, market value can be framed as a multiple of adjusted earnings (more on this later), a multiple of revenues, or a multiple of book value. Market value for privately held businesses can be affected by a variety of factors such as availability of credit financing or leverage, the overall level of private investment in the market, industry consolidation, public company valuations, and a host of other influences. In addition, private businesses typically are subject to what is called a "marketability discount," or a discount to the valuation for a similarly situated, publicly traded company because of the lack of liquidity inherent in a private company's stock. Put another way, it takes time to sell the stock of a private company, which makes its stock worth less than the stock of a public company that you are able to sell immediately in the public markets. Your advisor or investment banker should have access to databases that track private transaction information and he should use this information to help assess the value of your business.

Market value can also vary depending on the type of buyer. Some buyers are what we call "financial buyers," or buyers who are simply interested in earning a financial return on their equity or debt investment. Examples of financial buyers are private equity firms, venture capital firms, leveraged buyout firms, or private individuals looking to acquire a business. These buyers might be agnostic about the industry they invest in, or they may have developed an industry preference based on prior experience or investments.

Other buyers are "strategic buyers," or buyers within a specific industry looking to acquire similar firms either providing the same or a complimentary product or service. An example of a strategic buyer is Home Depot acquiring a building products distributor or a contracting business that uses the products Home Depot sells.

When the credit markets are forgiving and financing is relatively easy to obtain, financial buyers will likely be willing to pay more primarily because they can use leverage (or "other people's money") to enhance the returns they earn on their equity investment, even after paying a premium for an acquisition. Alternatively, when an industry is consolidating or industry participants are fighting for market share or are eager to gain scale by becoming bigger, strategic buyers will often be able and willing to pay a premium. This is due to the fact that these strategic buyers perceive they can capture operating efficiencies or other market advantages by growing through acquisitions.

As a result, the timing of when you take your company to market will often determine whether pursuing financial or strategic buyers makes more sense in terms of maximizing the value you receive for your company. Working with your team of advisors, you should be able to learn which buyers are most active and are willing to pay a premium for companies in the market, which should help dictate how you go to market with your business.

Whether strategic or financial, your buyer will also look to the prevailing market values to determine what they are willing to pay for your business. But how are market values determined? Market values simply reflect what willing buyers are currently paying to willing sellers in arm's length transactions. It is important to remember that market values can vary dramatically from company to company based on a number of factors, including the structure of the transaction, the health of the underlying business, the prospects for the specific industry, standard valuation "rules of thumb" used in specific industries, overall economic conditions, and other variables.

Buyers can come in a variety of shapes and sizes, and it is a little misleading to label them as either strategic or financial. We have seen strategic buyers (or buyers within an industry) who were not interested in paying any price over basic book value, and we have seen financial buyers who either had an investment in a particular industry or wanted to capture a market-leading position in a particular industry who paid more than fair market value for an acquisition because of its importance to their overall objectives. Whether your buyer is a strategic buyer or a financial buyer, your goal is for your buyer to place "strategic" value on your business. In other words, your objective should be to find that buyer, whether financial or strategic, who values your business for more than its current cash flow. This is where an objective assessment of your business from an outside advisor can be most useful.

Asset Approach. For some businesses, the best determinant of valuation (and in most cases the minimum value a seller should accept) is the fair market value of its assets minus liabilities. In industries that are highly capital intensive or require expensive equipment (crane operators, for example), or are valued primarily for their underlying assets (such as real estate companies or even homebuilders where the true asset is the underlying land value), a logical starting point for valuation is the net book value of its assets.

When reviewing any company's balance sheet, it is critical to review not only the book (or accounting) values of the assets and liabilities, but you must also methodically assess the fair market value of its assets and liabilities to ensure you are getting an accurate picture. For example, it is possible, even likely, that the fair market value of equipment assets is higher than the book (or accounting) value of these same assets. This is particularly true for companies that have taken advantage of special tax rules that permit accelerated depreciation of equipment. Let's go back to WidgetCo and look at its Balance Sheet:

WidgetCo Balance Sheet (in $)

Current Assets	1,000,000	Current Liabilities	500,000
Fixed Assets	2,000,000	Long-Term Liabilities	1,000,000
Accumulated Depreciation	(750,000)	**Total Liabilities**	**1,500,000**
Net Fixed Assets	1,250,000		
		Shareholders' Equity (Net Book Value)	**750,000**
Total Assets	**2,250,000**	**Total Liabilities & Shareholders' Equity**	**2,250,000**

Fair Market Value Analysis

Fair Market Value of Fixed Assets	1,750,000
Book Value of Fixed Assets	1,250,000
Difference Between FMV and Book	500,000

In the case of WidgetCo, for example, we can see that the Book Value of its Fixed Assets is $1,250,000, but when we assess Fair Market Value (or the value such assets would receive if purchased in an arm's length transaction between a willing buyer and a willing seller), we find that it is $1,750,000. When you hear reference to the Net Book Value of a company, this typically refers to the Shareholders' Equity of a company. In the case of WidgetCo above, we can see that the Shareholders' Equity is $750,000 (basically, Total Assets minus Total Liabilities). However, if we were to adjust for the Fair Market Value of WidgetCo's Fixed Assets, the Adjusted Net Book Value or Shareholders' Equity value for WidgetCo would increase to $1,250,000 (Book Equity plus the difference between Fair Market

Value and Book Value of WidgetCo's Fixed Assets).

Book Value also includes the value of Current Assets, as well as the value of Current Liabilities and Long-Term Liabilities. Current Assets include Cash, Accounts Receivable, Inventory, and other short-term assets (such as pre-paid amounts, deposits, etc.). In valuing Accounts Receivable, it is important to review the specific accounts, how old they are (commonly referred to as an Accounts Receivable "aging"), and whether or not they are likely to be collected in full or in part. In many cases, buyers and financing sources will discount the value of longer-aged Accounts Receivable to account for the risk that they will not be collected. In sum, the older an account receivable is, the less likely that it will be collected. Similarly, in the case of Inventory, it is critical to evaluate the Inventory count (for example, the number of widgets), the age of the Inventory items (is it still salable, or is it outdated to the point where it must be discarded?), and the condition of the Inventory. This type of analysis of Accounts Receivable and Inventory is equally important in determining the Adjusted Net Book Value of a company.

Similarly, a buyer will also review a company's liabilities, and should be very specific with respect to which liabilities he is willing to assume and in what amounts. Current Liabilities typically consist of Accounts Payable, Accrued Expenses, and other miscellaneous liabilities that are to be repaid in less than a year. Reviewing the aging of Accounts Payable, particularly over some period of time, will give a buyer some clues about a company's financial health (basically, whether they pay their bills on time or "stretch" their vendors by paying them over a longer period of time). A buyer will review the Accounts Payable to make sure they are accurate and that there are no other accounts payable that are not accounted for on the balance sheet for which they might be liable following acquisition.

Although typically not a large component of a company's balance sheet, a buyer should also determine whether the amount of Accrued Expenses accurately reflects the value of those expenses that should have been incurred for the month but have not been invoiced or included in payroll. A buyer will also review a company's long-term liabilities, which will include not only bank debt and other financing, but also liabilities for employee pension or benefit obligations, deferred income taxes (in the case of C-corporations), and other long-term liabilities. In addition, if a buyer is expected to assume any or all liabilities of the business (as in the case of a stock purchase), the buyer will want to understand what types of unknown or undisclosed liabilities could exist. For example, a company may have undiscovered environmental liabilities if it handles toxic chemicals, employment liabilities for terminated employees, or it might be subject to certain contractual obligations that it has not reflected on its balance sheet (pension obligations, projects not yet completed, and other similar liabilities).

"Goodwill" or Intangible Value. Once you have determined the fair market value of a company's assets and liabilities, you can determine the Adjusted Book Value of the company's Equity. As previously discussed, in the case of asset-intensive operations this Adjusted Book Value might be a reasonable starting point for valuation. However, a company also has assets that typically are not included or easily quantified on its balance sheet. These assets can range from key employees (for example, salespeople with key customer relationships), customer lists, patents, specific know-how, or brand name recognition in the market. Of course, these assets are only as valuable as the expected cash flow they are able to help generate. For example, in the case of WidgetCo its Adjusted Net Book Value is $1,250,000, yet it is able to generate EBITDA of $1,500,000 for which a buyer might be willing to pay $4-5 million. So, what accounts for this difference between the Market Value and the Adjusted Net Book Value? Typically, this difference is referred to as "goodwill," but can also be specifically captured in the intangible assets (customer lists, employees, backlog, brand recognition, patents, unique location, exclusive distribution arrangements, and other off-balance sheet assets).

When assessing the value of a business, it is important to understand not only valuation based on expected future cash flows, but a buyer should also be prepared to allocate value to the other assets in the business to the extent the Market Value exceeds Adjusted Net

Book Value. This allocation of value to specific assets will help a buyer more carefully evaluate the business and its risks. For example, if a large component of intangible value is ascribed to the key employees, the buyer may wish to enter into specific contracts with those key individuals to ensure they are retained for a reasonable period of time following a purchase. Understanding how to value goodwill and assess the risks associated with goodwill is a fundamental element of business valuation, and can make the difference between a solid acquisition and a poor investment.

A good way to determine whether a business has substantial goodwill or not is to examine the company's Return on Assets, or the ratio of net income to tangible assets (current assets [cash, accounts receivable, inventory] plus fixed assets [equipment, vehicles, other personal and real property]). The higher this ratio or percentage is for a company, the higher the value of its goodwill. In other words, if the Return on Assets is only 5-10% for a small to mid-sized business, this suggests the business does not have a large component of goodwill because the total tangible assets generate a substandard rate of return. Conversely, if the Return on Assets exceeded 40-50%, this suggests a large amount of goodwill because the return on tangible assets is very high. In determining the amount of goodwill, sophisticated buyers will typically rely more heavily on the Income Approach described below, as it captures all expected future cash flows, including cash flows generated from goodwill or intangible assets. This is also a more precise way to measure the value of goodwill than trying to assess the specific value of a customer list, proprietary process, patent, or other intangible asset.

Income Approach (Discounted Cash Flow/Capitalization of Earnings). The most sophisticated buyers of companies, in addition to reviewing a target's Market Value and Adjusted Net Book Value, will also perform a valuation using net income or cash flow as the economic benefit stream available to generate future returns. A Discounted Cash Flow analysis, in simple terms, states that the value of a business should be equal to the value of the free cash flow it will generate over the coming years, discounted for the time value of money according to the level of perceived market, industry, and spe-

20

cific company risk.

In some cases, where the stream of future earnings is highly pre-dictable, a buyer might use a Capitalization of Earnings approach, which simply applies a capitalization rate to the estimated future earnings to determine value. A Capitalization of Earnings approach is much more simplistic than a full Discounted Cash Flow analysis, and may not adequately reflect true business value. A buyer will typically use either Capitalization of Earnings or a Discounted Cash Flow analysis, but rarely both.

This can be a confusing topic for many non-accounting or non-financial types, so let's start with a simple example. Let's assume you were going to buy a business that you knew would operate for only two years (say this business operates a Haunted House, but the property lease for the Haunted House expires in two years). To keep our example simple, let's also assume that after expenses (including paying for your or someone else's time to run the Haunted House), this business is estimated to return $100,000 in cash flow in Year 1 and $100,000 in cash flow in Year 2. For purposes of our first exam-ple, after Year 2 there are no assets to sell and the business is fin-ished. Given what you now know, what should you expect to pay for this business?

In order to determine what you might pay for this business, there are two principal factors you should consider. The first is timing of the cash flow. In other words, because you can put the cash you would otherwise invest in an acquisition into a relatively safe in-vestment and earn, say, 5% annually, then at a minimum you would discount the value of your future receipt of the two annual cash flow sums of $100,000 by at least 5%. Think of it this way: if you were able to put $95,238 into a 1-year CD paying 5%, then in one year that CD would be worth $100,000 (or $95,238 multiplied by 1.05). Similarly, if you were to earn 5% over two years, then the amount you would have to put into the CD today to have $100,000 in two years would be $90,703 (which when multiplied by 1.05 for the first year and then again by 1.05 for the second year equals $100,000).

This 5% return threshold is sometimes referred to as the Risk-

Free Rate of Return, and most often refers to the current interest rate on U.S. Treasuries. So, at a minimum, you would not expect to pay more for the Haunted House's stream of two payments of $100,000 than you would have to invest to earn the same amount at a bank. As a result, you would immediately discount these two payments by what we refer to as a "risk-free" rate of return. When people refer to the "time value of money," they are referring to this concept: because your investment will earn a return by depositing it with a bank or other relatively secure investment vehicle, there is value in having money over a period of time.

The second part of your analysis should include an analysis of the specific risk factors of the targeted business or investment, including market risk, industry risk, and specific company risk. Consider the following: if the Haunted House had a contract with the local municipality to run the Haunted House for the city in exchange for a fixed fee paid by the city, regardless of how many people attended, this would be a less risky proposition than if you as the buyer took on all the risk of people attending. Just as junk bonds that are inherently more risky pay a higher rate of interest than highly rated "AAA" bonds, businesses or investments that are riskier than alternative investments will be comparatively less expensive to purchase. In other words, in our example, if the city guaranteed our fees from the Haunted House, we might be willing to pay more for the two $100,000 streams of cash flow than if we had to take on all the risk of people attending (the weather might be bad, a competitor might open up another haunted house across the street, etc.).

Conversely, you would expect to pay less if you were forced to assume the myriad risks related to operating a haunted house (liability for injuries, for example). To parse the analysis even further, you would need to assess what level of risk is involved in operating this particular haunted house as compared to the pool of all haunted houses (e.g., does it include particularly complicated exhibits that break often? does it have unique exhibits that appeal to a broad audience? will it require new exhibits to remain attractive to potential attendees?).

The challenge for every buyer is to determine what additional discount (on top of the discount attributable to the time value of money) should be applied to the expected stream of cash flows. For the sake of our example, let's assume that we would need to be paid 10% to take on the risk of the city contract, but we would need to be paid 20% in the event we had to absorb all the risk of attendance or non-attendance. In the former case, the total discount rate we would apply to the stream of cash flows is 15%, or 10% plus the risk-free cost of capital of 5% (see Example 1-A below), and in the latter case our total discount rate we would apply is 25%, or 20% plus the risk-free cost of capital of 5% (see Example 1-B below). As you can see, a buyer would be willing to pay $162,571 in Example 1-A, and $144,000 in Example 1-B for the same stream of cash flows based on the different assessment of the risk of those future estimated cash flows. Put simply, the higher the perceived risk the lower the ultimate valuation. Your transaction advisor is an invaluable resource in bringing wide experience with similar deals to help assess the various levels and nuances of specific risks inherent in the operations of any company.

Discounted Cash Flow Analysis: Example 1-A (in $)

		Year 1	Year 2
Net Cash Flow After Tax		100,000	100,000
Risk-Free Rate of Return	5.00%		
Specific Company Risk Factors	10.00%		
Total Discount Rate	15.00%		
Discounted Value		86,957	75,614
Total Discounted Value			**162,571**

Discounted Cash Flow Analysis: Example 1-B (in $)

		Year 1	Year 2
Net Cash Flow After Tax		100,000	100,000
Risk-Free Rate of Return	5.00%		
Specific Company Risk Factors	20.00%		
Total Discount Rate	25.00%		
Discounted Value		80,000	64,000
Total Discounted Value			**144,000**

Discounted Cash Flow models can become extremely complex, as you might expect, and assessing and quantifying risk is an inexact art at best. It is easy to be lulled into a false sense of security by reviewing a detailed, complicated spreadsheet. Don't let this happen to you. We know for certain that the forecast in a Discounted Cash Flow model is wrong; we just don't know whether it is aggressive or conservative. You must spend time with the underlying assumptions and test them for yourself if you truly want to understand a forecast model.

As a seller, you and your advisors need to understand how these models work, and how to argue the different assumptions buyers will use to reduce value. A good financial model will include not only the critical operating assumptions around revenues and expected costs, but will also account for different financing structures (e.g., more or less leverage or debt), different tax possibilities, and different asset assumptions. For example, does the business require heavy capital expenditures each year to stay in business? If so, you would need to account for those additional investments in your estimates of net free cash flow by year. In addition, a sophisticated buyer will run different scenarios (or what is commonly referred to as a "sensitivity analysis") which allow the buyer to understand what will happen to the business under different operating and financing conditions – this is particularly helpful for a buyer to be able to consider and anticipate different operating, economic, and specific market risks.

The combination of each of these different business forecasts will help a buyer determine what discount rate to apply to the expected stream of cash flows, and therefore determine what is a fair price to pay for the business. Obviously, once this baseline valuation has been established, the buyer will look to strike a better deal to further enhance his returns and reduce the risk of the investment.

One of the additional complications in a Discounted Cash Flow model is purposefully not accounted for in our first example above. This complication is the expected value of the business upon a future sale. In the case of our Haunted House, in Example 1, we assumed the business would be shuttered and would have no value after Year 2. To help illustrate the point of the value of a future sale of the business, let us assume instead that we will be able to sell the Haunted House after Year 2 for $175,000. Now, it is obviously critical to go through the analysis of how the sale price can be derived, but we will assume right now that the price is easily predicted. In this case, in addition to the value of the discounted operating cash flows, we also need to account for the discounted value of the future sale price.

In Example 2, note that with an expected discount rate of 15%, in addition to the value of the discounted operating cash flows of $162,571, we will also expect to earn a return of $132,325, or the discounted value of the $175,000 we expect to receive in Year 2. A buyer will also look at what percentage of the total value of investment is tied to the discounted value of the sale of the business. Where the percentage of total value in a deal is highly concentrated on the "exit" or "terminal" value of the business, it highlights even further the importance of understanding the dynamics and likelihood of a future sale at an assumed valuation. You don't want to be caught trying to unload the business to "dumber" money when market conditions deteriorate, as many people have learned in the past few years.

In this case, almost 45% is tied to the ultimate sale of the business, which is significant. This tells us we ought to look deeply into the market for Haunted Houses, the potential buyers, the expected length of the sale process, and other factors in order to give ourselves confidence in the ultimate sale and its price. Professional business buyers refer to this as defining your "exit strategy" – these types of buyers want to know who would be likely candidates to buy the business after 3-5 years. In some cases, we might even ascribe a higher discount rate or risk factor to the sale proceeds than we do to the operating cash flows, which we would need to factor into our ultimate analysis of value.

Discounted Cash Flow Analysis: Example 2 (in $)

		Year 1	Year 2
Net Operating Cash Flow after Tax		100,000	100,000
Discount Rate	15%		
Discounted Value of Cash Flow		86,957	75,614
Sale Price in Year 2			175,000
Discounted Value of Sale Price			132,325
Total Discounted Value			**294,896**
Percent of Total Value from Sale			44.87%

As you can see, unlike the simple Multiple of EBITDA or Multiple of Revenues calculations (using a multiple of a company's EBITDA or Revenues to come up with a value – see Chapter 6), the Discounted Cash Flow analysis is considerably more complex. However, you or your advisors will need to understand how these models are built so that you can anticipate the different factors that will affect valuation.

Of considerably more importance, however, are the insights you will gain into any business by understanding its financials and how operating assumptions impact not only financial performance but more importantly, the predictability of that financial performance. As illustrated by our Examples 1-A and 1-B, the major difference is not the future cash flow amounts. The difference between the two models is based on the risk, or variability, of those cash flows. If the expected cash flow from a specific investment is more predictable than the same cash flow from a less predictable source, then the former stream of cash flows will likely be worth more.

This is an important insight into business valuation that may seem obvious, but many people ignore: in order to make your business more valuable, you must make its cash flow more predictable and reduce the risk of future cash flows. As we will discuss in detail in later chapters, by doing nothing more than making your business more predictable (even if the total cash flow per year does not change), you can increase its value dramatically. Many small business owners do not understand this, but it is a critical factor in valuation. The absence of predictability can make or break a deal.

To illustrate the importance of predictability, let's look at an example based on a transaction we once explored in the telecommunications industry. The company generated over $10 million in annual revenues and earned over $2.5 million in net income and had grown significantly in the prior two years. On the surface, this seems to be a very attractive business, and its healthy net operating margins would appear to attract a fairly high purchase multiple. The business was engaged in the marketing and sale of telecommunications services on behalf of one principal telecommunications provider. In return for signing customers to carrier services contracts, the company would earn a commission from the carrier. In and of itself, this might not cause any immediate concern.

However, on closer examination we found that the company's contract with the carrier (and its commission plan) was subject to revision and/or cancellation on 30 days' notice. As a result, the predictability of the company's major revenue stream was challenging, and as buyers, we elected to pass on the opportunity because we did not value the stream of cash flows as highly as the seller did. As it turns out, the following year the carrier did indeed change the commission structure such that the company's revenues dropped to $5 million, and it ended up losing money while it reduced its cost structure. This proves the point that having a greater degree of predictability (less risk) will add value in a buyer's eyes, particularly because buyers do not have the same level of insight, knowledge, and understanding that a seller does about the industry or the seller's specific business.

In order to complete an accurate forecast of future cash flows, a buyer needs to spend a considerable amount of time understanding not only the specific business for sale, but also the overall industry and market conditions. Too often we see buyers compile rosy predictions in a spreadsheet, which often point to fantastic returns, only to see those same buyers lament their purchase because they did not anticipate operational, market, or economic challenges that every business faces.

In a solid Discounted Cash Flow model, the underlying assumptions for revenues, expenses, and the different balance sheet items must be thoroughly vetted and understood, with the best models including "sensitivity" analyses which help buyers understand how the business will behave under different assumptions (e.g., revenues or expenses are higher or lower, more or less capital investment is required, or working capital levels are higher or lower). As a seller, you and your advisors are well advised to prepare your own Discounted Cash Flow model ahead of going to market with detailed and well-reasoned assumptions. Having this type of model will not only force you to think more carefully about your own business, it will give you a leg up in negotiating with buyers when it comes to the value of your company.

Capital Requirements. One of the other important considerations that analysts and investors frequently overlook when completing a Discounted Cash Flow analysis is the level of capital investment a specific business requires either to grow or to maintain current revenue and profit levels. For example, we used to own a directional drilling company that drills horizontal holes for utilities of various types (electrical, gas, water, sewer, telecommunications, etc.). The drills required to perform this work are expensive, ranging in cost from $50,000 to over $500,000. For this business to grow, we had to purchase additional drills. In addition, to maintain revenue and profit levels, we frequently needed to invest to repair our existing drills and, over time, we would have needed to replace these drills, all of which requires capital.

A simple multiple of EBITDA analysis, or even a Discounted Cash Flow analysis that ignores the capital investment required to maintain existing revenue levels or to grow revenues, will miss a significant determinant of the ultimate cash-on-cash returns (return on investment). As a result, the buyer who ignores the costs of maintaining, replacing, or buying new equipment for growth will expect returns that are far greater than they actually will be and can consequently overpay for a company. As a seller, be prepared to discuss your own maintenance and growth capital expenditure requirements and to defend the useful life of your existing equipment, all of which will impact the overall value of your company.

Working Capital Requirements. Similarly, buyers need to have a detailed understanding of how the other balance sheet accounts will behave, and in particular how much working capital a specific business requires. For example, in a $12 million revenue business, the difference between having 30 days of sales outstanding in accounts receivable versus 60 days of sales outstanding in accounts receivable can require significantly more working capital (depending on the company's payables aging), which is a direct drain on cash flow and can require additional financing (with attendant costs and risks).

Conversely, a business that is able to use its vendors to finance growth may require less working capital. For example, many vendors will extend a growing company longer terms to pay accounts payable. In either case, it is important for a buyer to understand not only how these different accounts behave prior to closing, but even more importantly, they need to understand how these accounts will behave after closing (for example, is there some special deal with the vendors that a new buyer would not enjoy that would require additional working capital financing with a new buyer?). In preparing a detailed Discounted Cash Flow analysis, too many buyers focus on the income statement without having a detailed understanding of the balance sheet and how that will ultimately impact cash flow. Buyers who ignore this important piece will be disappointed and could lose their investment, and sellers who understand their own cash flows will be better prepared to defend their own valuation assessments.

CHAPTER 3

DECIDING WHEN TO HARVEST

I f you have done a thorough valuation of your business, and the expected value and returns are close to matching your financial and other requirements, then you can make the decision of when to go to market to harvest the wealth in your company. There are three different aspects to determining the appropriate time to go to market, two of which you have some control over, and one of which you will have little to no control over.

Market Timing. Many of our clients want to know when is the right time to sell their business to maximize its value. Just as it is difficult to pick the "top" or "bottom" of the stock market, it is nearly impossible to pick the ideal time from a market perspective to sell your company. Market valuations can and do fluctuate over time, sometimes dramatically as we have recently learned, due to changing public company valuations, tightening or loosening of credit availability, or the outlook for a particular industry segment.

We once represented a client in the homebuilding sector where the valuations were particularly attractive at the time we were engaged, but within one month, the overall housing market started to deteriorate, and within two months, the appetite for acquisitions of anything related to homebuilding dwindled, considerably reducing the number and valuation of the offers we received.

As a result, while an advisor can definitely give clients a sense for where the current market is based on prior transactions and what they are seeing in the market, it is challenging to predict where the market will be in six months. As a result, we encourage clients to think primarily in terms of the other two aspects that they can control: (i) personal timing for them and (ii) business timing for their company.

Notwithstanding the fact that we are always more optimistic about the prospects of selling a business in a market upswing, we have also had enough experience with solid businesses to know that even in tough markets, good businesses will sell. Valuations may fluctuate based on the economy, the stock market, the availability of credit and other factors, but we have sold businesses even in the midst of very challenging market conditions, including one transaction in December of 2008, three months after one of the worst stock market meltdowns in history. The steps we outline in this book are of even more importance in a tough market: proper positioning and buyer identification can mean the difference between getting a deal done and having to wait for a better market.

Personal Timing. The right time to sell a business is different for each business owner from a personal perspective. Every business owner has specific financial and other goals associated with his business, and has different personal considerations that drive a decision whether to sell or to continue to operate the business. These personal considerations can include the state of an owner's health, marital changes, the desire to spend more time at home, or the desire to start a new business. In all cases, however, as a business owner you will be well served to think through your own personal timing and what will help you generate the largest financial and non-financial return from your business, whether you decide to sell or continue operating.

As you review your own goals, objectives, and lifestyle, ask yourself and your advisors how the timing of your decision to sell can add to or detract from these considerations. It is often difficult to predict the future and how you might react to no longer owning your business, but if you can articulate your goals and objectives clearly, and analyze those in light of either selling or keeping your company, you will at least start to clarify how the timing of your decision to sell might help or hurt your overall objectives. Completing this analysis will also help you when the time comes to "pull the trigger" on a specific offer from a buyer – you will already know in advance what your financial requirements are, and you will be equipped to evaluate a buyer's offer in light of those requirements, reducing the anxiety associated with selling your company.

In our Seller's ToolKit, we include a Seller's Personal Needs Interview Questionnaire, which you might find useful. In it, we list a variety of thought-provoking questions designed to help business owners think through their decision to sell. The questions we include are focused primarily on the qualitative aspects of selling and what happens after a sale, but you will also want to talk with your financial advisor to review your post-closing financial requirements.

Business Timing. Unlike market timing, which is hard to predict, and personal timing, which can be challenging to quantify, business timing is comparatively straightforward. As we previously discussed, selling an ailing or shrinking business is often a tough time to sell if you are trying to maximize value. Conversely, selling a growing and healthy business often leads to realizing full value at closing. Similarly, if the key qualitative factors in your business (employees/management, customers, strategy, and organization) are not where they need to be, spending the time to fix them prior to going to market with your company will lead to better value creation, independent of the timing of the sale of your business. This can sometimes result in millions of dollars of additional value creation at closing, which obviously merits attention and planning.

On occasion, we run across companies where the current team has brought the business to a stage where the company needs to be managed differently going forward, and probably by different managers who have experience growing similarly situated companies. This often occurs when a start-up has matured to the point where it requires more professional management with experience growing larger companies.

As the owner, it is no doubt challenging to be objective about your own and your team's capabilities as they relate to this next phase of growth for your company, but that is where candid dialogue with your advisors can help you to see your business more realistically. Most business owners and entrepreneurs have never met a challenge they did not think they could conquer, so it is often difficult for them to consider the possibility that their company might be better managed by someone else, yet this can often be the case. Managing a business growing from $10 million to $100 million is fundamentally different from managing a start-up – start-ups require managers to wear multiple hats, be creative in attacking new markets or incumbent providers, manage tight cash flow, and generally define the culture and direction of a business.

Conversely, managing a larger, growing business means building a management team with more specialized expertise, developing and managing more clearly defined and repeatable processes, and managing more sophisticated financing needs. As a result of the different management skills and expertise required by businesses in different stages of their life cycles, the ideal timing for a sale of a company may coincide with the need for this type of management change. Indeed, there are several private investors who specialize in making investments in companies in transition because they can bring the required skills to a business and help capture value for their contributions.

The best timing to go to market with your business can also be influenced by the type of transaction you are contemplating. For example, the sale of 100% of your company might dictate different timing for a sale than a sale of less than 100%. Selling 100% of your company's equity usually means you are not going to be managing the business much longer, which may or may not fit your goals and desires. Conversely, in many cases private equity firms have a strong interest in buying less than 100% of a company to keep the current management team focused on continued growth.

As an owner selling less than 100%, having a solid private equity partner can help provide additional capital to grow and allow you to capture a "second bite at the apple" when you and your new partner sell 100% of the company, hopefully at a higher valuation than the initial purchase by the private equity firm. We have seen examples of owners selling less than 100% and actually making more money on the second sale than on the first sale. Obviously, this requires selecting the right private equity firm as your partner, which in turn requires a lot of due diligence on your potential bidders.

In any case, in our experience there is always a market for well-run business with solid management teams in decent industries. By focusing on those things you can control, most business owners can still control their own destiny when it comes down to selling their company, but it does require careful and thorough planning by you and your advisors.

CHAPTER 4

DRIVING VALUE OUTSIDE THE FINANCIAL STATEMENTS

I ncreasing the value of your business is not as challenging as you might think, although it may take some time. Valuation really deals with the perception of risk, and the perception of risk can be influenced in a variety of different ways. It is important to know that there are things you can do right now to increase the value of your business that have little to do with driving more revenues or higher profits.

When we discussed how businesses may be valued in Chapter 2, we focused primarily on the financial results of WidgetCo. While it makes our examples easier to understand, it oversimplifies how sophisticated buyers really look at companies. While many company owners may believe value is mostly financially driven, a sophisticated buyer will look beyond the financials of a business to more thoroughly understand how the business behaves and performs, which involves an assessment of several qualitative factors in a business.

As we discussed above, one of the most significant determinants of business value is the predictability of earnings (or level of perceived risk in future earnings), which comes from a variety of factors that may not be immediately apparent in a company's financials. In order to fully analyze a company, we use a simple framework we call Value Drivers, which assesses a company's strengths or vulnerabilities in five principal areas: Financial Value, Organizational Value, Customer Value, Employee Value, and Strategic Value. With respect to each of these different Value Drivers, the primary path of inquiry is to assess a company's level of risk, which can increase or decrease a potential buyer's perception of value in your company.

Financial Value. We have already discussed the principal elements of Financial Value above, which are based primarily on the discounted value of the company's future earnings. However, there are other elements of Financial Value that are more qualitative in nature that can add to or detract from a company's perceived risk. These elements include: whether a company follows fundamental and industry-accepted accounting practices, the extent to which a company's financial statements are externally reviewed, and the level of organization and discipline within a company's financial team and processes.

As you might expect, sophisticated buyers are very familiar with accounting rules and regulations, all the way from basic matching of costs and revenues to more sophisticated accounting concepts affecting project accounting. If a company does not follow basic accounting rules (sometimes referred to as Generally Accepted Accounting Principles, or "GAAP"), then the financials are inherently suspect and will require much more time and energy from a buyer to understand completely. Not having GAAP-based financials increases the perceived level of risk for a buyer, and consequently will lower the subject company's valuation from a skeptical buyer. For example, we have had more than a few clients whose businesses were primarily project-based, and as buyers dug into their financials, they found that project revenues and costs were not matched appropriately, which delayed the closing of the respective transactions several months. In cases where the buyer could not get completely comfortable with the financial statements, the buyer lowered the ultimate valuation to account for the additional perceived risk.

Similarly, the extent to which a company's financial statements are externally reviewed can also enhance or detract from a company's valuation. An external review of a company's financial statements is done by an independent accounting firm. The type of evaluation completed by the outside accounting firm can range from a simple *compilation*, a more thorough *review*, or a complete *audit*. A compilation is the most basic external review, and involves the accounting firm simply taking the existing company's internal financial statements and compiling them into a presentable format. The accounting firm doing a compilation will not do any verification of the accuracy of the financials or test any of the accounts to make sure the financial statements they are compiling are accurate. In this regard, a compilation is not of much use to a buyer because the buyer will in essence do their own compilation as they build their financial model.

A review is more thorough than a compilation, and will involve a modest amount of testing and evaluation of the financials by the accounting firm. While not as thorough as an audit, a review, particularly for "stub" periods (periods of time less than a full year), is of some value to a buyer and will certainly help get a buyer more comfortable with a company's financials.

A full audit is the most comprehensive form of review an accounting firm can do. An audit requires the accounting firm to test and validate each balance sheet account, and to stand behind the financials as an accurate and complete portrayal of a company's financial statements. In other words, an accounting firm signing an audited set of financials tells the buyer that the financial statements are correct and complete from the accounting firm's perspective, and subjects itself to potential liability if the financial statements presented in the audit are incorrect. An audit will also include detailed footnotes explaining how a company accounts for certain things, which is of particular value when trying to understand a company's financials in total.

As you might expect, from a buyer's perspective, not all audits are viewed equally. For example, an audit from one of the larger, national accounting firms will be of more value to a buyer than an audit from a sole practitioner because the larger firm has more resources to stand behind the results of the audit if the audit is found to be incorrect, and the larger national firm is generally better regarded than a sole practitioner.

Presenting a buyer with financial statements audited by a reputable firm will reduce the level of perceived financial risk from a buyer's perspective, and therefore increase a buyer's valuation. However, as an owner of a business, whether it is for sale or not, you can also benefit from having an accounting firm review or audit your financials, which is why we always recommend to our clients that they have their financial statements audited prior to us taking their company to market.

When an outside accounting firm reviews or audits your financial statements, it can also uncover problems with your internal financial controls that have a direct bearing on the profitability of your business and the accuracy of the financial statements you are using to manage your business. There are several elements to having solid financial controls that are beyond the scope of this book (including concepts like segregation of duties, among others), but in general, the tighter your financial controls, the more accurate your financial statements are likely to be and the less likely you are to experience problems like fraud and waste. As a result, having an audit or even a review completed will give you very valuable feedback on how disciplined and organized your financial and accounting functions are within your business.

Needless to say, a company with tight, documented financial controls will be perceived by buyers as having less risk than a company with loose, undocumented financial processes. In addition, uncovering accounting issues through an audit ahead of taking your company to market allows you to fix these issues before they become a potential issue for a buyer. We have been involved in a number of transactions where the audit was performed at the request of a buyer and uncovered significant accounting issues, which in all cases delayed or killed the transaction. Fixing these issues prior to taking your company to market will better ensure a smooth, quick transaction.

Another important element to Financial Value is the consistency of a company's earnings over time. For example, a business that generates $500,000 in free cash flow on a very consistent basis is likely to be worth more than the company that makes $1.5 million one year, loses $500,000 the next, and makes $500,000 the next year. The reason for this is simple: the more consistent a company's earnings (especially if they are growing over time), the more reliably a buyer can forecast future earnings, which results again in a perception of decreased financial risk and a higher valuation.

Organizational Value. The second element of our Value Drivers analysis involves the level of organization and discipline within a company, or what we refer to as Organizational Value. This can apply not only to internal records, but also to the general appearance of a company and its environs. We like to use the example of going to a five star restaurant, sitting down, and noticing a dried piece of pasta is stuck on your knife. No matter how good the food is, your impression of the restaurant will undoubtedly be negative.

Likewise, if a company's records are in disarray, we advise clients to clean them up and organize them well before considering going to market with their business. This is important not only to prepare for the due diligence process that will ultimately occur prior to a transaction, but also because it helps to organize the business and its operations, which is a good thing for any business regardless of whether or not it goes to market. Having organized records and presenting them in a logical format to a potential buyer also creates an initial positive impression with the buyer, which cannot be underestimated in determining value.

Put yourself in the shoes of a buyer: Which would you feel more comfortable with: a company whose records and documents are well-organized and easy to navigate, or a company that struggles to put everything together or find original copies of critical agreements? In the former, the buyer will see less risk and will perceive that the rest of the business is also well-oiled. In the latter, the buyer will see lots of risk based on the sloppiness with which the company operates, which will almost certainly lead to decreased value for the seller.

In a similar vein, make sure that the appearance of your company – your offices, warehouse, trucks, etc. – is clean and neat. For all the same reasons, having an organized and clean physical appearance creates the impression of orderly operations and a measure of pride in the business, which is attractive to buyers. What they say about first impressions is absolutely true when it comes to buyers.

Customer Value. The third element of our Value Drivers analysis is Customer Value. Let's assume Company A and Company B have identical financial statements and earnings. Company A has one major customer who comprises 90% of its business, and who is currently experiencing an industry downturn unrelated to the industry of Company A, but that could put pressure on Company A's pricing or on the volume of purchases coming from Company A's customer. Conversely, Company B has no customer that accounts for more than 5% of its overall revenues, and with respect to its largest customers, they come from diverse industries and have different risk exposures. It doesn't take too long to figure out that Company B is worth a lot more than Company A because of the significant risk to Company A's future earnings should something happen to Company A's major customer.

On occasion, we will hear from owners that they don't understand how such a solid relationship between Company A and its top customer can be a bad thing, to which we respond not only with the example above, but also with the advice that they simply need to find more customers like this one! This is also where valuation between a buyer and seller can diverge significantly. The owner of Company A, being very knowledgeable about its major customer's industry, management, and buying patterns, can assess the risk of its customer diversity with more accuracy and more reliability. Conversely, a potential buyer of Company A has limited information, which serves to increase the level of risk in the mind of the potential buyer such that the buyer's valuation for Company A may be significantly below the owner's valuation.

For example, we once considered acquiring a local contracting business that had very healthy profits (the company had consistently made $1 million in each of the prior four years), but was dependent on two principal customers. We valued the business at a little over $2 million given this risk and the fact that the contractor depended heavily on new construction for its revenues, but the owner (as it turns out, rightfully) valued the company at over $5 million.

The owner had a high level of confidence based on what he knew was happening in his specific market with his two specific customers – he knew the business would stand to make over $2 million in the coming year. In hindsight, the owner was "right" and we missed out on a decent opportunity, but we are like many buyers – we tend to assess risk with the most pessimistic view.

In sum, if your company is dependent on only a few customers for the majority of its revenues (what is called high "customer concentration"), you should start developing your marketing and sales plans to get at least some customer diversity if you are going to increase the value of your business. This will also allow you as the owner to sleep better at night, independent of whether you decide to sell or not.

With respect to a company's customer base we also try to determine how many are long-term customers, and if the top ten customers rotate from year to year. In many project businesses, the list of top customers can change from year to year because customers may only have one or two projects with the company in a given year. In this case, we look for the referral sources the company uses to generate new business to see if there is loyalty among them. Even if the nature of the business might not permit true customer loyalty, such as with government contractors, we want to know whether the business has any elements of "recurring" revenue based on its lead sources or other factors. In general, customer or referral source loyalty is a positive indicator with respect to the overall value proposition of the company, and also lowers risk levels going forward to the extent that you can count on revenues from either of these sources.

Although it may be obvious that the quality of a company's customers is a significant determinant of valuation, too often buyers neglect to really understand the true nature of the customers and how they might behave following a sale of the business. Sophisticated buyers will dig into understanding the company's customer base and really focus on the company's larger customers to get a thorough sense of the likelihood they will remain long-term customers after a sale. In some cases they might find that the company's top customer is a friend of the owner's and that after a sale a buyer may not be able to rely on them as a long-term customer.

In other cases, a buyer might find a company's top customer is having financial difficulties of their own or was recently acquired or changed management, all of which can have an impact on their viability as a customer going forward. For any material customer, a buyer will go through this analysis, even to the extent of talking directly with the customer if the seller will allow it. This is often a sticking point with sellers, although if done carefully near the end of the due diligence process we have seen it accomplished with good results. As a seller, be prepared to discuss your top customers and think through how to get buyers comfortable with their ultimate longevity with your business.

Employee Value. If you can focus on the predictability of earnings as being a key determinant of valuation, then you will quickly grasp how buyers look at a business in general. For example, if a buyer is looking at a business in which the owner is also the key operations manager and salesperson, the buyer is right to suspect that the company's future potential earnings are going to be a lot less predictable when the owner's financial incentives are fundamentally different or the owner is no longer involved. This is the case with many small businesses, and as a result, smaller businesses without a deep bench of management talent trade for lower valuations than larger businesses that are not as dependent on the owner. A naïve buyer may believe he can do better than the seller, but a sophisticated buyer understands that successful business owners typically are doing everything they can to be successful, and more importantly, that the selling owner usually has a lot more information and knowledge about the industry and specific company than the buyer.

Indeed, there are several management books for owners of small businesses that emphasize the importance of the owner developing a bench of managers who can run the business for the most part without the day-to-day involvement of the owner. We are strong advocates of this approach for owners because it helps give an owner flexibility: if an owner wants to sell his business so that he can have more free time to spend with his family or pursue his hobbies, in our opinion he should not wait to sell his business to create this flexibility. By developing a team that can run his business without his direct involvement, he will create the flexibility to have his desired free time, which means he is able to sell his business at any time he chooses. We refer to this as "exiting before you sell."

Too many times we see business owners desperate to leave their businesses who have not taken the time to build their team. As a result, they are apt to take the first reasonable offer they receive for their business, which usually means they have left money on the table. For some business owners, building a strong team is very challenging. They have been successful precisely by being "in control" and not letting their employees make decisions (and therefore make the inevitable mistakes). However, whether a business owner ultimately decides to sell or not, building this strong second tier of management is critical to their ultimate exit strategy.

In short, increased value for your business comes from flexibility and having options. By creating the ideal working environment for yourself right now, you reduce the pressure to sell at any particular time and allow yourself the option of continuing to run the business under acceptable conditions if you do not receive the right offer for your business. As a corollary, building a deep team to operate your business means that your business will be much more attractive to a buyer, and as a result, will be worth more. A potential buyer who has to assess the risk of your departure on the future earnings potential of your business will typically overestimate that risk, and as a result underestimate the value of your business. You are better off taking this element of risk off the table by having an experienced, competent team that will continue to operate your business after your departure much in the same way they did when you owned the business.

Savvy buyers will also look beyond your senior management team to the next layer or two of employees in your business. For example, does your business have a low or high degree of employee turnover? What are the skills and competencies of your employees? What types of relationships do your employees have in the market?

A company with long-tenured, talented employees who have demonstrated success in the past is a very positive quality for a company. If a company has high turnover relative to its specific industry, it usually indicates something is amiss within the company that will warrant further exploration. A buyer facing high turnover has to immediately find new employees and loses whatever institutional knowledge the departing employees had. A high level of employee turnover may also raise questions about the company's culture or value system, which can also be red flags. It might, however, simply be something inherent in the industry (for example, call centers typically have a higher level of employee turnover than most other businesses).

Similarly, if a company's employee base is less experienced, this further heightens the risk associated with the operations of the business while these employees get up to speed. Recall that a buyer wants to reduce variability in earnings, and having solid, seasoned employees that have exhibited loyalty to the company reduces that risk. Conversely, a buyer will also want to explore whether the loyalty of the employees is due to factors that might disappear after a potential sale. For example, it might be that the members of the senior management team (or even the entire employee base) have an equity stake or some interest tied to the sale of the company that will vest and be paid out upon a sale. This may be what they have been waiting around for, and after a sale, they may be at risk of departure. Or it might be that the employees are very loyal to the owner on a personal level because he or she has treated them very well by paying them above-market wages, using large bonuses, or giving other benefits a new owner might not be willing to accommodate.

In any case, it is prudent for a buyer to really understand the motivations of the key employees and ask lots of questions prior to consummating a transaction so that the buyer can understand their risk of departure. Conversely, as a seller, you should plan for this type of inquiry from a buyer and be prepared to alleviate a buyer's concerns about the competence and continuity of your management team and employees.

Strategic Value. Customer diversity is important, but buyers will also place a higher valuation on companies that have certain elements of what we call Strategic Value. Strategic Value can include the nature and predictability of a company's revenue stream, brand value, position in the market, and other qualitative factors. Looking at a company's revenue stream, it is important to understand the nature of customer purchases – specifically, whether customers buy one time from the company, or they are repeat buyers.

For example, we own a few contracting businesses, some of which focus on residential projects and some of which focus on commercial projects. The residential projects are largely one-time deals – once a residential project is completed, that customer is unlikely to need similar services for quite some time. Commercial projects, on the other hand, are typically contracted through general contractors with whom our company hopefully enjoys long-term relationships in which we are repeatedly invited to bid on or negotiate new projects with them. These relationships are ideally more recurring in nature, where we hope they are customers over a period of years.

We also own a telecommunications services business in which our company gets paid a commission on a monthly basis based on the overall revenues our customers generate. While this business takes longer to get off the ground, it enjoys a much more predictable stream of recurring revenues, which consequently is more valuable and reduces the risk of this business going forward. To the extent you can focus your business on repeat customer relationships, your business's revenues and profits will be more predictable, which consequently increases business value.

Another key determinant of whether or not your revenues and profits will be predictable going forward is the power of your company's brand. A well-known company with a good reputation for superior products or services has a greater potential for predictable revenues and profits than a lesser-known company or a company with a questionable reputation. For example, even in the case of our old residential contracting business, by having a well-known company name with a solid reputation in the market, notwithstanding the fact that our contracts are one-time transactions, we could expect to earn significant business by virtue of having a well-known brand.

Companies develop a strong brand over time by delivering consistently solid products and services, or they invest heavily in marketing and advertising to create better brand awareness. Placing a value on this brand, or even assessing whether it is well known or not, is a tricky proposition. For the largest brands this is pretty straightforward, as there are national companies that test these brands in the market.

For smaller companies in niche industries, it is more challenging to assess the value of the brand, although with some work it can be done. By talking with existing and potential customers (how did they come to find out about the business? what do they think of it?), you can get a sense of how recognizable a brand is and what reputation the company has. You can also look at a company's financials to see how much they are spending on advertising and marketing (and how much they have spent in the past) to determine how much a company has invested in their brand and what audience the company is targeting. Brands can also increase in value to the extent they have been protected by a registered trademark such that other companies cannot use them.

Another component of Strategic Value depends on the level of market competition. Some companies enjoy more predictable cash flow because they have exclusive territories for the sale of their products or services. Most products or services face competitive offers in the market, but if your company does not have to "meet itself in the market" by competing against identical product or service offerings, it helps margins and reduces the unpredictability in revenues or cash flow that comes from direct competition. For example, many franchisees have exclusive territories that can have value beyond what their financials might show (although typically they are committed to paying a royalty for this privilege, which can impact valuation in the opposite direction by draining cash flow).

Similarly, if a company has a patent on a particular process or product that allows it for a set period of time to sell that process or product exclusively (typically 17 years in the United States), it will enjoy pricing power when it comes to its patented products or services. For example, many drug companies enjoy quasi-monopoly status with respect to their drugs before their patents expire, which is why newer drugs are more expensive than older drugs, the patents for which have expired (meaning they will face competition from generic drugs that are able to use identical formulas).

Utilities are a good example of companies whose earnings are relatively predictable. Because of a lack of competition, utilities generally are regulated monopolies, meaning they are the only provider in a particular geographic region for a specific service (electricity, gas, water, sewer, etc.). The most significant variable for a utility's earnings is the underlying usage rates for its specific service and the utility's cost to provide that service. In the case of electricity and gas utilities, their earnings will largely depend on weather, as unusually hot or cold weather will result in higher gas or electricity usage. Because they are regulated utilities, the prices they can charge their customers, and therefore the ultimate profit they can generate, are regulated. As a result, the real risk for utilities is underlying influencing factors (weather, supply prices, and other variables), and substitution (solar energy, for example). As a result, the earnings of utilities are relatively predictable, although because they do not grow significantly from year to year (they basically grow with population growth), the typical valuation for a utility is relatively conservative.

Value Drivers Summary. As highlighted above, savvy buyers will go well beyond a simple review of a seller's financial statements. Sophisticated buyers will delve deeply into a company's financial processes and controls, its organization, its customers, its employees and management, and the specific strategic factors that either enhance or detract from value. As a seller, you will want to understand each of these elements in your own business, preferably far in advance, so that you can proactively address any weaknesses or vulnerabilities well before you take your company to market. In some cases, it can take years to enact meaningful change in terms of your company's specific Value Drivers, so the earlier you start, the more successful and rewarding your results will be.

CHAPTER 5
UNDERSTANDING FINANCIAL STATEMENTS INSIDE & OUT

Most successful business owners are pretty financially savvy, even if they don't know all the rules of accounting. Indeed, a business owner who does not understand financials, particularly his own financials, is not likely to last long in business. However, business owners sometimes struggle to understand the details behind the formal rules of financial accounting and cash flow statements, which can be to their detriment when selling their company.

At a minimum, business owners should understand their own financial statements inside and out. This includes the income statement, the balance sheet, and the cash flow statement. In particular, you need to understand the key drivers for each of the different line items for the income statement, balance sheet, and cash flow statement, why they have changed over time, and why the ratio of one line item to another may have changed from period to period. Most business owners already have an innate sense of this information; it just may not be organized very well in their minds or on paper.

The following is a very high level overview of the different components of a company's financial statements. We have also provided some suggestions for lines of questioning to better understand what the financial statements can tell you about how a company is performing. These are merely suggestions and are not designed to be comprehensive in any way.

The Income Statement. The Income Statement, sometimes referred to as a Profit and Loss Statement (or P&L Statement), can reveal several important facts about a company's operations. Beginning with a company's "sales" or "revenues," the "cost of sales" or "cost of goods" is then subtracted to calculate "gross margin," from which "operating expenses" are subtracted to calculate "operating income." Interest expense, income taxes and "unusual expenses or income" are then subtracted (or added) to operating income to determine "net income after tax."

Beginning with sales or revenues, a solid financial analysis will determine whether a company is growing or shrinking and why, which will then lead to further questions about the different components of revenue. For example, some types of revenue, such as revenues that are guaranteed by contract or are recurring in nature, are more valuable than others, and growth in those desired areas can lead to a better valuation. In addition, understanding the level of revenues from a company's top customers can help you understand whether a company's revenues are too concentrated with a few customers, which can increase the perceived risk of the company's future revenues if one or more of those customers stops buying.

After reviewing sales or revenues, a financial analyst should then look to cost of sales or cost of goods sold. Cost of sales or cost of goods sold represents the direct costs of generating revenue. For example, in a contracting business, these costs would include the direct labor and direct material costs related to a specific project, but would not include general overhead costs that are not directly allocable to a specific project. Subtracting cost of sales from revenues results in a company's gross margin or gross profit, which is important to trend over time both in absolute dollars as well as a percentage of revenues. These trends will help to uncover whether the company is experiencing pricing pressures or cost increases, and whether those trends can be expected to continue. It may also uncover shifts in sources of revenue – for example, if margins are deteriorating, it might suggest that the proportion of lower margin revenues is growing in relation to higher margin revenues, which may or may not be a concern. In short, it is critical to understand why a company's gross profit percentages have changed over a period of time if you are going to develop a reasonable forecast model.

Once gross profit is calculated, subtracting operating expenses (general overhead expenses that include sales, marketing, advertising, general and administrative and other costs) generates operating income. Again, trending the different expense line items, as well as the overall levels of operating profit in absolute dollars and as a percentage of revenues, can reveal important facts about how a company is performing and whether it may need to increase operating expenses to generate further revenue growth. Some operating expenses are fixed (like rent) while others may vary according to the level of sales (such as sales commissions). After determining operating income, subtracting interest expense and income taxes will result in net income after tax. A buyer developing a forecast for a target company's profit and loss statement following closing will need to account for its own tax structure and capital structure. For example, if the buyer is going to increase the amount of debt on the target company's balance sheet to fund a portion of the purchase price, he will need to account for this interest expense as well as what principal amounts are due following closing.

The Balance Sheet. A company's balance sheet can also provide several clues about the financial health and performance of the company. In particular, trending the different balance sheet line items, as well as understanding the ratios of different balance sheet accounts to different income statement line items (as we provide in Appendix C), can help you better understand a company's operating results and can lead to further substantive questions that are critical to fully understanding the company.

On the "left" side of the balance sheet are the company's assets, which are typically divided into current assets and fixed assets. Current assets include items like cash, accounts receivable, inventory, and deposits. Fixed assets include automobiles and equipment, furniture and fixtures, real estate, and other long-lived assets. On occasion, you might see goodwill as an asset on a company's balance sheet. While more involved than what we can discuss here, goodwill is typically generated after an acquisition in which the purchase price exceeds the book value of a company's net assets.

With current assets like accounts receivable and inventory, it is important to understand the aging of these accounts. Older accounts receivable and older inventory are often worth less and are harder to convert to cash than younger accounts. With accounts receivable, the longer an account goes unpaid by a customer, the less likely it will be ultimately converted into cash. Similarly, older inventory can sometimes go "stale" where it is not salable or is only salable at a lower price. In either case, it is not sufficient to simply look at the book value of receivables or inventory. A solid financial analysis requires a deeper level of understanding in order to adequately assess their true value, and to understand what they suggest about the operating condition of the business.

Fixed assets like automobiles and equipment must also be carefully assessed both for their age, as well as their likely useful life and working condition. If a buyer needs to shortly replace aged equipment or equipment that is not in working order, it will adversely impact the free cash flow available from the acquired company, which will in turn negatively affect value.

On the "right" side of the balance sheet are liabilities and shareholders' equity. Like assets, liabilities are classified as current liabilities and long-term liabilities. Current liabilities are generally liabilities that will become due within one year, such as accounts payable, accrued liabilities, accrued expenses, working capital lines of credit, and the short-term amounts due on long term debt.

A close examination of current liabilities such as trade payables or accounts payable can also yield clues about what is happening with the underlying business. If trade payables are relatively current, that can suggest the company has sufficient cash to pay its vendors on time or that its vendors are very strict with respect to payment terms, either of which has implications for cash flow going forward.

Similarly, an examination of long term liabilities is particularly important if a buyer is expected to assume them following closing. Even if a seller will handle a company's long term liabilities following closing, watching the trends in long term liabilities will help you understand how the business cash flows. Significant borrowings suggest the business is not generating cash, which is important in any valuation discussion.

The Cash Flow Statement. Often given less attention than the Income Statement or Balance Sheet, the Cash Flow Statement is of critical importance in any evaluation of a company's financial and operating performance. The Cash Flow Statement is essentially a reflection of the cash coming in and going out of the business for a specific period of time. Oversimplified, it can be derived from the Income Statement and Balance Sheet by taking net income, adding back non-cash expenses, and then subtracting any increase in assets and adding any increase in liabilities. Developing a true Cash Flow Statement is complex, and you should talk with your accountant or transaction advisor to develop a comprehensive view of your own cash flow. However, running a cash flow analysis on your own business on a monthly basis (or even more frequently) will help you better understand the fundamental operating performance of your company.

By diving deeply into your financial statements and being able to answer these questions in an organized fashion, you put yourself ahead of many business owners who may not have this level or type of understanding of their business. This analysis will also uncover insights into your business that you may not have otherwise noticed before. You can use your outside accountants and advisors to help you better understand your financials and where profits and cash flow might be leaking away.

As mentioned above, we don't have enough time or space here to explain all the details behind financial statements or all the rules for financial accounting, but it would be worth your while as a business owner to become familiar with basic accounting. There are several business books that outline basic accounting for those business owners who want to expand their knowledge of financial statements. If you are planning to sell your company, you will serve yourself well by learning some basic accounting because this will likely be the language of buyers and you definitely want to be able to "talk their talk."

In particular, you should work to understand how the Income

Statement and Balance Sheet work together to create your Cash Flow Statement. For example, it is possible for a company's Income Statement to show net income of $1 million, yet for its Cash Flow Statement to show that it generated only $500,000 in cash flow. This difference between net income and actual cash flow can be due to a company's capital investments, significant growth in accounts receivable, or other factors that are important to a potential buyer. As a result, although the company may have earned $1 million, a buyer might not be willing to pay based on net income when actual cash flow is only one-half of net income. The reverse may also be true: a buyer may want to focus on net income as the key valuation metric when cash flow exceeds net income. To position your business in the best light possible as it relates to both net income and cash flow, you need to have a basic grounding in these fundamental measurements of business performance.

Financial Ratios. In addition to understanding financial statements, sophisticated buyers will also look at the health of a business as measured by specific financial ratios. In Appendix C: Financial Ratios, we have defined and explained some of the more prevalent ratios used by financial analysts to understand a business, particularly as they relate to the Balance Sheet. As a seller, you would be well advised to run these ratios on your own business to understand where you have strengths and weaknesses, and where you can improve your business prior to a sale.

By incorporating some of these key financial ratios and metrics into your regular internal financial reporting and understanding how these measurements impact value, it will allow you to be more proactive and strategic in your decision making. Many buyers appreciate this type of reporting as it suggests not only that you are managing your business strategically and with an eye toward key operating metrics, but it also helps them understand your business better, which can reduce perceived risk. Most small to mid-sized businesses are woefully lacking in financial and operating information that is readily available to help managers make decisions, so by having this information ready and in a format where buyers can quickly understand trends and indicators, you will likely increase the perceived value of your company and will be in a better and more informed position to make important decisions along the way.

CHAPTER 6

YOUR BUSINESS IS WORTH A MULTIPLE OF...

E arlier we discussed how to use the discounted cash flow method to value a business. In our opinion, this is the best and most thorough way to value a company, yet in the market you will often hear buyers, sellers, and business owners talk of "multiples." This could be a multiple of earnings (net income), EBITDA (earnings before interest, taxes, depreciation, and amortization), revenues, or book value (don't worry – we define all of these terms below in more detail). A savvy buyer or seller familiar with these multiples may be able to strike a favorable deal if they are able to understand the difference between a true discounted cash value and a "rule of thumb" multiple. As a result, it is important for you to understand the differences between these methods of valuation and how they will often result in different valuations.

As a seller, you want to understand each and every possible way your business can be valued and be prepared to direct buyers to the most appropriate, and most advantageous, way to value your business with all of its unique characteristics. Doing this requires a deep understanding of your own company and its financials, as well as the different ways buyers value businesses and use their expertise to drive the best bargain. After all, if the potential valuation of companies in your industry ranges from three times EBITDA to six times EBITDA, what distinguishes the company that sells for three times EBITDA from the company that sells for six times EBITDA?

Multiple of Revenues. In the case of private companies, particularly companies with a limited operating history or those operating in emerging growth industries such as software or the Internet, you may hear buyers and sellers refer to valuation in the context of a Multiple of Revenues. In this case, business value is expressed simply as a multiple of some period of revenues (either the current year's expected revenues, next year's expected revenues, or the trailing twelve months' revenues). Again, sophisticated buyers do not stop here – they will take the valuation derived by the Multiple of Revenues approach and compare it with their overall purchase analysis and return on investment calculations based on their operating assumptions.

Be careful with any valuation based on a Multiple of Revenues because, without further detailed financial analysis, this type of valuation can get buyers into trouble when they ignore important fundamental operating cost assumptions. Internet company valuations in the late 1990's probably best illustrate the difficulties in valuing businesses with metrics other than free cash flow. Internet companies were often valued based on revenues, number of "clicks," number of unique "eyeballs," and other valuation approaches that had little bearing on the ability of these companies to truly generate a financial return on investment. As a result, buyers of these companies (or their public shares) suffered tremendous losses because they ignored important fundamental valuation analysis.

Multiple of EBITDA v. Net Income. Perhaps the most commonly expressed market value metric is the "price to earnings" ratio, or the "earnings multiple." In the public markets, most valuations are based on a multiple of net income after taxes, or what you might have heard referred to as the price-to-earnings ratio or the short-hand "P/E Ratio." This ratio is simply the market value of a company's equity divided by its after-tax earnings.

In the private markets, you will commonly hear reference to an "EBITDA Multiple." EBITDA refers to a company's earnings before interest, taxes, depreciation, and amortization, and unlike a public company P/E Ratio, the EBITDA Multiple refers to a company's enterprise value (which comprises a company's total capital structure – equity plus debt) divided by the company's EBITDA for the previous twelve months. This can be pretty confusing, so let's walk through an example with a private company, WidgetCo, to clarify:

WidgetCo Income Statement (in $)

Revenues	10,000,000
Cost of Sales	6,000,000
Gross Margin	4,000,000
Operating Expenses	2,500,000
Depreciation & Amortization	500,000
Operating Income	1,000,000
Interest Expenses	200,000
Net Income Pre-Tax	800,000
Income Taxes	320,000
Net Income After Tax	*480,000*
Earnings Before Interest, Taxes, Depreciation, and Amortization ("EBITDA")	*1,500,000*

WidgetCo Balance Sheet (in $)

Current Assets	1,500,000
Fixed Assets	1,500,000
Total Assets	*3,000,000*
Current Liabilities	500,000
Long-Term Liabilities	500,000
Total Liabilities	*1,000,000*
Shareholders' Book Equity	*2,000,000*
Liabilities and Shareholders' Equity	*3,000,000*
Total Shares Outstanding	1,000,000
Book Equity Value Per Share	*$2.00*
Per Share After-Tax Earnings	$0.48
Market Price (Publicly Traded)	$6.50
Total Market Equity Value	*6,500,000*

Ratios and Multiples

Market Equity to Book Value	3.25
Market Equity to After-Tax Earnings (Price to Earnings or P/E Ratio)	13.54
Market Enterprise Value to EBITDA (EBITDA Multiple)	4.67

Looking at WidgetCo's Income Statement, we can see that WidgetCo had revenues of $10,000,000, and that after deducting its Cost of Sales and all Operating Expenses, its Operating Income is $1,000,000, to which we add the non-cash charges Depreciation and Amortization ($500,000) to determine WidgetCo's EBITDA. In this case, WidgetCo's EBITDA is $1,500,000, or a respectable 15% of WidgetCo's Revenues of $10,000,000.

Note that WidgetCo's EBITDA of $1,500,000 is significantly different from WidgetCo's Net Income after Tax, which is $480,000. WidgetCo's Net Income after Tax is essentially WidgetCo's EBITDA, minus WidgetCo's Interest ($200,000), Income Taxes ($320,000), and Depreciation and Amortization ($500,000).

Now, let's look at WidgetCo's Balance Sheet, as this is important to understand how the different market ratios are calculated. In this case, WidgetCo's Shareholders' Equity (or what accountants refer to as "Book Equity" as it is derived directly from a company's accounting records or books) is $2,000,000. Note, however, that a company's Market Equity Value can differ dramatically from a company's Book Equity Value (Market Equity value is typically higher than Book Equity, although not always). In the case of WidgetCo, its price per share on the publicly-traded market is $6.50, which, when multiplied by the 1,000,000 shares of WidgetCo stock that are outstanding or issued, equals a Market Equity Value of $6,500,000, which is 3.25 times WidgetCo's Book Equity Value (this is referred to commonly as a "Multiple of Book Value").

In the context of publicly traded companies, the most common ratio used by analysts is the P/E Ratio. In this case, Price refers to the

Share Price (in this case, $6.50), and Earnings refers to the Net Af-
ter-Tax Earnings per Share of the company (in our case, $0.48 per
share). So, taking the Share Price ($6.50) and dividing by the Per
Share Net After-Tax Earnings ($0.48 per share), we get a P/E Ratio
of 13.54. Note that this is significantly higher and different from
WidgetCo's EBITDA Multiple.

In the context of private companies (and sometimes when analyzing public companies), you might hear a reference to the prevailing
EBITDA Multiple. The EBITDA Multiple is determined by dividing
a company's Enterprise Value by its EBITDA (earnings before interest, taxes, depreciation, and amortization expenses) for the past
twelve months. A company's Enterprise Value is different from its
Equity Value. Enterprise Value equals a company's Market Equity
Value plus its Long-Term Liabilities. Enterprise Value is also known
as the market value of all invested capital, where invested capital includes both debt capital and equity capital. For example, when you
buy a house for $100,000 using $20,000 of your own money as a
down payment and $80,000 as a loan from a bank, $100,000 represents the Enterprise Value of the house, $20,000 represents the Eq-
uity Value you have in your house, and $80,000 represents the
Liabilities associated with the house.

In our case above, WidgetCo's Market Equity Value equals
$6,500,000 as we showed above, but its Enterprise Value is equal to
$7,000,000 (Market Equity Value plus Long-Term Liabilities). So,
when you look at public companies, understand that the P/E Ratio is
very different from an EBITDA Multiple. We often hear these terms
used interchangeably, but they are not the same thing. Typically,
once a buyer determines the overall Enterprise Value they are willing
to pay for a company (as a result of the buyer's calculation using the
EBITDA Multiple approach), if they are expected to assume any
Long-Term Liabilities (which can take the form of debt or other
long-term liabilities), they will subtract the value of such Long-Term
Liabilities from the overall Enterprise Value to come up with Equity
Value, or what they are willing to pay for the company's Equity. In
WidgetCo's case, if a buyer were expected to assume WidgetCo's
Long-Term Liabilities of $500,000, then the price it would be willing

to pay WidgetCo's shareholders for WidgetCo's Shareholders' would equal the Enterprise Value ($7,000,000) minus WidgetCo's Long-Term Liabilities of $500,000, or $6,500,000.

So, why do public equity analysts use a P/E Ratio versus an EBITDA Multiple? In some respects, these are simply shorthand ways to value a business. Some buyers use EBITDA as their key earnings metric because it eliminates non-cash charges (depreciation and amortization), removes expenses that are dependent on capital structure (interest) and the owner's specific tax situation (taxes), and can reflect a company's true earnings power prior to imposing a specific capital structure.

Many investors, however, argue that interest and depreciation matter, as they are true costs incurred to run a business. Warren Buffet, for example, disdains any analysis of EBITDA because it ignores real business costs for which an investor must account. In the case of private companies, however, a buyer's assumptions around capital structure (and hence how much interest expense a company will incur under new ownership) can be very different from the seller's capital structure. However, depreciation is a real expense because capital equipment must be maintained and replaced over time, and it is likely that these expenses will be similar under either the buyer's or seller's ownership.

As a result, while an EBITDA Multiple is helpful to understand where market values are because that is how buyers quickly evaluate businesses, no analysis is complete until a thorough analysis of net income after tax has been completed and a buyer's return on investment calculation has been done. In short, wise buyers may use an EBITDA Multiple as an initial test for valuation, but they will also look at every other valuation metric to check their work, including what we view as the most important analysis, an evaluation of Cash-on-Cash Return as well as Return on Investment.

One other reason analysts use a P/E Ratio in the context of a public company is that public investors are buying a piece of an existing business which has an existing capital structure and tax basis that the shareholder must accept. This structure does not typically change after their purchase of shares. Conversely, a buyer for a private company has the ability to change the capital structure, which allows them to use their own assumed capital structure (which may change the company's costs for taxes, interest, depreciation, and amortization). As a result, private company buyers should look at a company's earnings prior to deducting these costs and insert their own costs to determine their specific return on investment.

Cash on Cash Return and Return on Investment. Ultimately, the only investment measurement that is likely to matter to a buyer is the return on their investment of capital. Different investors have different ways in which they will characterize their returns, and some investors may have a different definition for Cash on Cash Returns or Return on Investment than we have here. Regardless of how different investors may characterize or label their returns, however, it is important to understand the difference between the various ways returns can be calculated, regardless of what they are called.

In the case of WidgetCo, let's assume it is a private business that is expected to have income in future years that mirrors its current income statement (in other words, it will earn $1,000,000 in operating income, and have EBITDA of $1,500,000). Let's assume that a private buyer decides that it will value the business at an EBITDA Multiple of 3.5 times, which means in this case, they are willing to pay $5,250,000 (3.5 times $1,500,000) for the business. Let's assume the buyer expects the shareholders of WidgetCo to assume WidgetCo's Long-Term Liabilities of $500,000, in which case the net Purchase Price to WidgetCo's shareholders is $4,750,000 (which equals the gross Purchase Price of $5,250,000 minus the $500,000 in Long-Term Liabilities the buyer must assume).

Most buyers will use a combination of equity financing and debt financing to purchase a business. Typically, the equity financing will come from the buyer or its investors, and the debt financing will be provided either by a third party, such as a bank or other lender, or the seller (seller financing).

In our example, let's assume the buyer decides to finance the purchase of WidgetCo with $3,150,000 in equity (60% of the Enterprise Value) and $2,100,000 in bank debt (40% of the Entity Value) at a 10% interest rate. For our example, let's assume the debt financing is provided by a bank to make the example easy to understand. Further, let's assume the bank debt is amortized over 7 years (in other words, the principal is amortized or paid back over 7 years). Let's also assume that new capital expenditures equal half of depreciation expense (which may or may not be a reasonable assumption, depending on the life cycle of the business, the condition and useful life of its hard assets, and how it has been accounting for depreciation). Here, now, is what WidgetCo's Income Statement and Cash Flow Statement would look like:

WidgetCo Purchase Analysis: Example 1 (in $)

Income Statement			Purchase Assumptions	
Revenues	10,000,000		Purchase Multiple	3.5
Cost of Sales	(6,000,000)	(60%)	EBITDA	1,500,000
Gross Margin	4,000,000	40%	Purchase Price	5,250,000
Operating Expenses	(2,500,000)	(25%)	Percent Leveraged	40%
EBITDA	1,500,000	15%	Debt Financing	2,100,000
Depreciation and Amortization	(500,000)	(5%)	Equity Investment	3,150,000
Interest Costs – Year 1	(210,000)		Interest Rate	10%
Pre-Tax Net Income	790,000		Term	7
Taxes	(276,500)	35%		
Net Income after Tax	513,500			
Cash Flow Analysis			Return Calculations	
Net Income after Tax	513,500		Cash on Cash Return	17.21%
Plus Depreciation	500,000		Return on Investment	16.30%
Minus Capital Investment	(250,000)			
Principal Repayment – Year 1	(221,352)			
Free Cash Flow	542,148			

In the previous example, the Returns on Investment are calculated as follows: Cash on Cash Return is the Free Cash Flow (cash flow generated after taxes, interest, capital investment, and loan repayments) divided by Equity Investment. Note that in this case we have assumed WidgetCo is a C corporation, which incurs income taxes at the entity level (as opposed to an S corporation or limited liability company, both of which are not taxed at the entity level). In this case, Cash on Cash Return is Free Cash Flow of $542,148 divided by the Equity Investment of $3,150,000, or 17.21%. Return on Investment, however, is defined as Net Income after Tax divided by Equity Investment, or in this case, Net Income after Tax of $513,500 divided by $3,150,000, or 16.30%.

As you can see from the example above, the Free Cash Flow of $542,148 on an Equity Investment of $3,150,000 equals 17.21%. However, if you include the fact that the investors have also paid down $221,352 in debt (and correspondingly built up Shareholders' Equity by the same amount), the returns increase to 24.24% on the initial Equity Investment, which is a solid after-tax internal rate of return, although some investors require higher expected returns before they will invest. In this case, Cash on Cash returns are slightly higher than the Return on Investment because of the fact that capital expenditures are only half of annual depreciation expenses, and because of the fact that the principal amortization payments are slightly less than the difference between depreciation expense and capital expenditures. Hopefully from this example you can see how important it is to understand the capital needs and capital structure of a business going forward.

A sophisticated buyer will run a detailed financial model which, while it may start with EBITDA, includes the full income statement, balance sheet, and statement of cash flows to determine their expected return on investment. In private businesses, it is not unusual for investors to expect returns of 20% or more to compensate them for the higher level of risk inherent in smaller, privately held (illiquid) businesses. In the case of larger transactions where lenders may be more willing to participate in transaction financing, potential buyers may be able to increase their equity returns by increasing the amount of leverage or debt they use to complete an acquisition, although this can significantly increase the risk to the equity holders, particularly when times are challenging (as we have seen in late 2008, for example).

In the case of WidgetCo, if the buyer chose to increase the debt portion of its purchase financing to 70% (instead of 40%) as we show in Example 2 below, the Cash on Cash Returns are about the same at 17.38% (the initial investment is lower, but the interest and principal costs are higher), but its Return on Investment for its Equity increases to 26.10%, and its internal rate of return (accounting for the fact that the business is paying down principal on its debt) increases to 41.98%.

It is important to remember, however, that increasing the amount of debt used in a purchase also increases the level of risk in the investment. In this case, interest costs and principal repayments increase from $431,352 per year to $754,865. As a result, if WidgetCo were ever to experience a downturn (whether due to internal or external factors), its risk of default on its debt would increase.

Increased equity returns due to increased leverage are inherently riskier returns. As an illustration of this risk, private equity firms that used upwards of 80-90% leverage in 2006 and 2007 when financing was relatively cheap and easy are now experiencing the pains that such leverage can bring when operating results fail to meet expectations. Banks understand this, and typically restrict the amount of debt a buyer can use and may also require personal guarantees from the buyer to better ensure repayment of the debt.

WidgetCo Purchase: Example 2 (Higher Leverage) (in $)

Income Statement			Purchase Assumptions	
Revenues	10,000,000		Purchase Multiple	3.5
Cost of Sales	(6,000,000)	(60%)	EBITDA	1,500,000
Gross Margin	4,000,000	40%	Purchase Price	5,250,000
Operating Expenses	(2,500,000)	(25%)	Percent Leveraged	70%
EBITDA	1,500,000	15%	Debt Financing	3,675,000
Depreciation and Am-ortization	(500,000)	(5%)	Equity Investment	1,575,000
Interest Costs – Year 1	(367,500)		Interest Rate	10%
Pre-Tax Net Income	632,500		Term	7
Taxes	(221,375)	35%		
Net Income after Tax	411,125			
Cash Flow Analysis			Return Calculations	
Net Income after Tax	411,125		Cash on Cash Return	17.38%
Plus Depreciation	500,000		Return on Investment	26.10%
Minus Capital Invest-ment	(250,000)			
Principal Repayment – Year 1	(387,365)			
Free Cash Flow	273,760			

Adjustments to Earnings. Most private companies that make money attempt to minimize taxes (usually legitimately but on occasion close to the edge of propriety), typically by increasing expenses. This may mean the owners pay themselves more than a typical salary, or the owners use the company to handle expenses that otherwise might be more personal expenses (such as auto expenses, salaries for their children or other relatives, insurance, tickets to sporting events, and other items). When a sophisticated seller presents his business to the market, he will want to "re-cast" the earnings of his business to represent what the company's financials would look like in a "normal" operating environment. These adjustments are what you may hear referred to as "add-backs." On occasion, sellers will also attempt to "normalize" earnings by removing one-time events (litigation, for example) that have had an adverse impact on historical earnings.

As either a buyer or seller, you should be careful about making too many adjustments to historical earnings – or at least you should have a very clear understanding of why such an expense will not recur under new ownership. One of our favorite sayings is that "life is a series of one-time events." Business is no different – every business will have its share of positive and negative surprises over the course of time, and to arbitrarily eliminate just the negative surprises is to suppose the future business will be immune to what afflicts every business from time to time, which is dangerous. Sophisticated buyers understand this and will rightly push back at sellers who excessively "dress up" their earnings.

Some sellers, for example, will argue for an add-back of all the owner's compensation. In the case where the owner is not truly involved in the operation of the business, this may make sense, but both buyers and sellers should look carefully at the underlying responsibilities and activities of the owner before deciding that such compensation is not required going forward. For example, an owner may argue that his salary should be added back to earnings, yet when looking beyond the surface, it is apparent that the owner is the key salesperson or the key operations person. Even if the owner departs, these responsibilities must be filled by someone, and typically the replacement is not willing to work for free. Our final word on add-backs: they have a place in reviewing a company's historical financials and in understanding the true earning power of a company, but be sure to carefully think through why they would be one-time or non-recurring expenses, and make sure to balance them out with one-time events that may have happened on the positive side. Significant add-backs translate to increased risk for the buyer, and this will likely be reflected in the buyer's perception of overall value.

As an example, a seller's proposed adjusted financial statements might look like the following:

Reported Net Income	**$500,000**
Adjustments:	
Depreciation	$50,000
Owner Salary/Benefits	$150,000
Donations	$25,000
Denver Nuggets Tickets	$25,000
Property Taxes	$10,000
Total Adjustments	$260,000
Adjusted EBITDA	**$760,000**

A savvy buyer will look hard at each one of these adjustments to make sure they are not going to be expenses going forward under new ownership. For example, as we discussed above, depreciation is a real expense if the new buyer has to buy new equipment or repair existing equipment. Similarly, even if the current owner/manager leaves following a sale, the new buyer will have to either work himself or hire another manager at market rate, which means all or some of this adjustment is likely to be trimmed. For donations and the Denver Nuggets tickets, the seller might argue that this was for his personal use and preferences, but a buyer will want to know how often these were used for customers or for key referral relationships that would be important to future revenue generation. Finally, when taxes are used in the context of calculating EBITDA, it refers only to corporate income taxes – in this case, property taxes are not an appropriate adjustment because these expenses will continue to be incurred following closing (whether as the future owner of the subject property or even as a tenant where these costs are passed through).

Comparable Transactions. Whether value is determined using a Multiple of EBITDA, Multiple of Revenues, or other valuation approach, you still need to do the fundamental research into comparable transactions or valuations in the market to determine how the market currently values businesses such as yours. In the case of publicly traded companies in the same industry as yours, with a little work you can determine how companies in your industry that have similar characteristics are valued. With online tools such as Yahoo Finance, Edgar Online, and a host of other financially oriented websites (www.cnbc.com, www.bloomberg.com), you should be able to determine how companies in your industry are valued from a variety of different perspectives (PE Ratio, Multiple of EBITDA, or Multiple of Revenues).

This process can be more challenging, however, if there are few or no public comparables in your industry. For example, there might not be public companies that fit the profile of your business exactly (this is generally the case for many small contracting businesses). In this case, you will need to access private company databases such as MergerMarket, Pratt Stats, and others. In most cases, access to these databases requires a subscription, and the better and more comprehensive databases are typically expensive, particularly for individual searches. In addition, for databases that require some sophistication to search and analyze, you may need the help of a valuation expert or someone skilled in researching and analyzing private company transactions to properly locate and analyze transactions in your industry. If you are preparing to sell your business or are in the early stages of considering a sale of your business and need to understand its value, we highly recommend employing a valuation expert. For fees starting at five to ten thousand dollars, an expert can prepare a comprehensive valuation report that will include private market comparable transactions and an analysis of how these compare to your specific business.

CHAPTER 7

T oo often when discussing business value we find business owners caught up in the overall valuation number. While important, it is also critical to understand the potential structure of the transaction as well as the underlying capital structure of a business. Understanding capital structures can help you better assess the risk level associated with different types of equity and debt, and can prevent entering into a riskier transaction than you anticipated.

<u>Availability of Financing and Valuation</u>. As you might expect, when credit or financing for transactions is easily available and relatively cheap (we will discuss later what this means), valuations for businesses typically increase. Businesses go typically up. In the case of larger acquisitions where a buyer is not expected to personally guarantee debt financing, the amount of available financing and its cost can have a significant effect on valuations in the market. Recall in our examples in earlier chapters that increasing the leverage in an acquisition can increase equity returns under the same operating conditions. If an equity investor's risk does not include the risk of the debt financing (in contrast to instances where the equity investor is required to personally guarantee the debt financing, as happens in many smaller transactions), then the equity investor will be tempted to increase equity returns by increasing the amount of debt financing employed.

Assuming similar operating conditions, this means an equity investor using more leverage can pay a higher price for an acquisition and still earn similar returns on investment. Therefore, when credit is easily available, valuations are likely to increase. This was particularly true in the three to four years leading up to the dramatic market correction in late 2008 and early 2009. Private equity firms utilized significant cheap debt financing to push target company valuations to ever higher levels until these firms' sources of financing dried up, after which company valuations contracted significantly. There is widespread anticipation that many of these highly leveraged companies will go bankrupt because the overall economic and market conditions have deteriorated, making it even more challenging for these companies to stay current with their debt payments.

If you are a seller to a buyer utilizing significant amounts of debt, you must understand the consequent pressure such debt places on a company's operations, and the risks it poses to you if you continue holding any equity or subordinated debt. Having a high degree of leverage can also be detrimental to your employees, customers, and suppliers. A company that experiences operating challenges that is also highly leveraged may have trouble paying vendors on time, may have to restructure operations and reduce costs (including terminating employees), and may put the equity holders at significant risk of not earning any return or worse, eliminating any value at all in the company's equity. Therefore, make sure you understand how capital structures work and how different operating scenarios can affect the ultimate financial and other outcomes you expect from a sale. We explore these concepts at a high level below.

Cost of Debt. You may hear analysts refer to "cheap" capital on occasion, but exactly what does this mean? In one respect, it is pretty simple. The most obvious cost of debt financing is the interest rate a debt provider charges to use debt financing. On a relative basis, lower interest rates mean less expensive capital. In the mid-2000's, as interest rates decreased and derivatives allowed banks to decrease the risk of lending (or so they thought), bank and debt financing sources became increasingly eager to lend more money, which consequently lowered interest rates these financing sources charged. This cheap debt resulted in some very rich acquisition prices using very large amounts of leverage, which are coming back to haunt these same investors and the operating businesses they purchased.

There is another potential cost of debt that sometimes is underrated. On occasion, and particularly in the case of subordinated debt (more on this later), a debt financing source will not only demand interest payments for the use of the debt capital, but it may also demand warrants, or options, in the company to purchase equity at a fixed price. These are sometimes referred to as "equity kickers" and they have the effect of diluting existing equity holders to the extent that the warrant or option holder can purchase equity shares at a price that is lower than fair market value. This happens when the per share value of the company increases beyond the option or warrant "strike price" (the price at which the warrant or option holder can purchase the underlying equity shares). Obviously, the higher the value of the equity, the greater the impact of this dilution to the other equity holders.

To illustrate this, let's compare two situations where debt financing is provided and in one instance, the debt financier does not require any warrant coverage, and in the other instance, the debt financier requires a warrant for 10% of the company's equity at the then-current fair market value for the company of $10,000,000. These types of sophisticated financial instruments are typically seen when dealing with financial buyers such as private equity groups, mezzanine lenders, or hedge funds, but may also be used by other types of buyers.

WidgetCo Warrant/Option Dilution Example

Current Fair Market Value of 100% of Common Equity for WidgetCo	$10,000,000
Warrant Coverage Percentage	10.00%
Exercise Price for Warrant (at Current Fair Market Value)	$1,000,000
Fair Market Value of 100% of Common Equity for WidgetCo in 5 Years	$15,000,000
Fair Market Value of Warrant Equity (10% of FMV of Common Equity)	$1,500,000
Minus Exercise Price	($1,000,000)
Equals Value of Warrant	$500,000

As you can see from the example above, a 10% warrant can have a significant impact on the cost of debt financing overall. The $500,000 value of the Warrant above comes directly out of the remaining equity holders' pockets, which affects how "cheap" debt truly is. You may also hear reference to "mezzanine financing," which is financing that typically sits between secured financing and equity holders, similar to subordinated debt, but usually carries warrant coverage with it.

Capital Structure. The capital structure of a company is comprised of the different forms of capital invested in the business. Capital can come in an almost unlimited variety of shapes and sizes, but in general, it is comprised of equity capital and debt capital, each with different variations. A company's existing capital structure and the buyer's proposed capital structure can have an impact on the business's likely success going forward and how buyers may look at a particular transaction. Although companies can take various legal forms (S corporation, C corporation, LLC, LLP, Partnership, among others), the capital structures for companies often follow a similar pattern. What follows below is a high-level description of the different components of a company's capital structure. This should help you better understand how equity and debt can be structured. A company may have all or only one or two of the components listed below (and sometimes creative combinations of two or more of these components), so it is important that you understand how these different components can take shape in a transaction. We will only address this in a summary format. You should spend time with your tax and legal advisors to understand your own specific situation in detail and how it would impact transaction structure and ultimate valuation.

Capital Structure Component	Priority in Liquidation	Level of Risk	Description
Secured Senior Debt	First	Lowest	Least Risky First Claim on Company Assets Secured by Company Assets Banks are Typical Providers
Secured Debt	After All Senior Secured Debt	Second Lowest	Priority Over Equity and Non-Senior Debt Secured by Company Assets Second in Line After Senior Can Carry Warrants, But Not Usually
Subordinated Debt or Mezzanine Debt – Can Be Secured or Unsecured (as in the Case of Trade Creditors)	After All Secured Debt	In the Middle	Priority Over Equity, but Subordinated to Other Debt Often Carries Warrants Trade Creditors Can Fall Into This Category at Times
Preferred Equity	Second to Last	Second to Highest	Priority Over Common, Subordinated to Debt Often Carries Dividend Often has Liquidation Preference Converts into Common to Allow Share in Upside Potential
Common Equity	Last	Highest	Subordinated to All Debt and Preferred Highest Potential Upside

Investors in a business, whether they are equity or debt investors, trade expected upside returns against the security level of their investment. By this we mean that equity holders whose returns are paid only after every other component of the capital structure is paid will enjoy the highest level of upside, but also bear the highest level of risk. In the four scenarios in the following table, we start with the overall value of the company (which in our case ranges from $1.5 to $10.0 million). Then, in order of priority of claim on the assets of the business, the different classes are paid out. In this case, when the business is being liquidated, the Senior Secured Debt holders are fully paid out their $1 million, the Secured Debt holders get 50 cents on the dollar, and the remainder of the company's stakeholders get nothing. Conversely, where the business is worth $10 million, every class of debt and equity is paid out, and the holders of Common Equity get the remainder, or $6 million. To keep things simple, this table assumes there is no participation right for the Preferred Equity, and that there are no warrants or options outstanding.

Participation Levels In Sale or Liquidation

	Initial Invest- ment Level	Bankruptcy or Liquidation of Assets	Sale of Business: Scenario 1	Sale of Business: Scenario 2	Sale of Business: Scenario 3
Value of Company	5,000,000	1,500,000	4,000,000	6,000,000	10,000,000
Senior Secured Debt	1,000,000	1,000,000	1,000,000	1,000,000	1,000,000
Secured Debt	1,000,000	500,000	1,000,000	1,000,000	1,000,000
Sub-Ordinated & Trade Debt	1,000,000	-	1,000,000	1,000,000	1,000,000
Preferred Equity	1,000,000	-	1,000,000	1,000,000	1,000,000
Common Equity	1,000,000	-	-	2,000,000	6,000,000

* These scenarios assume the preferred dividends have been paid – if not then these amounts would be paid to the preferred equity holders (plus any conversion premium they may have) prior to the common equity holders.
** These scenarios assume no warrant coverage – in the event of warrant coverage the Common and Preferred-Equity Holders' value would be reduced or diluted.

As you can see from this table (which is admittedly very simplistic to illustrate the point), as the level of risk increases in the capital structure components, the levels of expected return increase, provided the company's valuation is high enough.

In sum, the value of your business or the business you may be looking to purchase is dependent on a variety of factors. Given the importance of this aspect of deal making, we strongly suggest that if you do not have a financial or transactional background you enlist the support of someone who does. Too many times we find naïve buyers or sellers who either leave money on the table or, worse, make a terrible decision that comes back to haunt them later. Spending the money now on solid advice and understanding all the different factors that can impact the value of a transaction is money very well spent. More importantly, understanding how the buyer's proposed capital structure will affect your remaining equity or debt investment in the business, your customers, employees, and suppliers, is a critical component of your evaluation of a buyer's offer. Don't neglect this important consideration.

CHAPTER 8
GOING TO MARKET – THE SALE PROCESS OVERVIEW

So, you've decided to sell your company, you know the probable value of your company and the likely alternatives for deal structures, you have evaluated your financial needs after closing, you have worked on the non-financial aspects of your business to enhance its value, and you are committed to a clear post-closing plan. What should you expect from the actual process of going to market?

We have already discussed part of the first and most important step, Preparing for Sale. However, there is more work to be done before going to market. In addition to understanding the value of your business and your specific needs, you will need to now work with your advisors to present and position the business in the most favorable light possible, understanding that any materials you present will need to be thoroughly supported and substantiated.

A typical transaction will follow a fairly standard process and timeline, provided everyone is cooperating and information is exchanged on a timely basis. First, as we mentioned above, your investment banker will want to spend time with you to learn your business in a fairly high degree of detail. They will request and review your documents, financials, and other materials, conduct industry research on their own, and interview you and others you select. This is an important part of the overall process because if your advisor is well informed, it will save you untold hours later in the process by avoiding repeated questions from multiple buyers. In addition, having extensive and in-depth knowledge of your company will help your advisor best position your business in the market with respect to both your company's strengths and weaknesses.

Once your advisor or investment banker has spent time learning your business, he will also spend time researching the market through his own channels and databases, learning more about your competitors, customers, suppliers, and operating metrics. These are all useful pieces of information to properly position your company for sale, which we explore in more detail in subsequent chapters.

After reviewing your business and doing fundamental research, your advisor or investment banker will then begin to draft a document that describes all aspects of your business: financials, marketing, sales, operations, management, employees, suppliers, competition, the overall market, and other salient aspects of your company and its performance. This document is sometimes referred to as "the book" and is typically distributed only to potential bidders that have executed a nondisclosure or confidentiality agreement. We discuss the book in more detail in Chapter 10.

In parallel, your advisor or investment banker should begin to develop the list of potential bidders he will contact regarding their interest in acquiring your company. There are several different methods for compiling this list of potential bidders, which we discuss in Chapter 11.

Once your investment banker has completed the book and compiled the list of potential bidders (both of which you should approve), he will begin contacting bidders to solicit interest in your company. This can take as little as three to four weeks or as long as six to twelve months, depending on the nature of your business and the state of the market.

If all goes well, your investment banker will have generated interest from three to five (or more) bidders and will conduct either a formal or informal or "soft" auction so that you can select one of the bidders with whom to sign a letter of intent, which will include all the material terms of the contemplated acquisition. After signing the letter of intent, you will then be engaged in due diligence with a buyer, as well as contract negotiations on the final transaction documentation. All of this we discuss in more detail in Chapter 12.

In sum, the transaction process is like any other business process. If it is carefully and thoughtfully planned, it will work. If it is not managed with a disciplined and well considered plan, it will cause a lot of headache for you as the business owner. As a result, it is critical that you and your advisors plan your exit event well ahead of time, and anticipate different potential outcomes so that you are prepared for any contingency.

<u>A Note of Caution: Pay Attention to Your Business</u>. Other than how to accurately value a business, the deal process is probably one of the murkiest and most confusing areas for business owners. If you are not familiar with the process, it can seem tedious, time-consuming, sometimes boring, infuriatingly slow at times, and expensive. On the one hand, you have attorneys, accountants, and advisors working with you to build your book, after which you will be involved in presentations, meetings, and other distractions even ahead of starting to negotiate a deal. On the other hand, you are expected to continue to operate your business on a daily basis to ensure it continues to grow and prosper. When we first meet with clients, one of the things we emphasize is that throughout the sale process, as important as it is, it is even more important for an owner to stay focused on the operation of his business so that it stays healthy and vibrant. Too many times we have seen business owners get wrapped up in a deal or the sale process, only to see their business begin to struggle, which in turn makes a sale more challenging and can adversely impact value.

If you are like most business owners, the closest experience you have had to selling a business is either the sale or purchase of a home or other real estate, or perhaps a major sales opportunity with one of your customers. Unlike a sale of real estate, in which you pay a large fee for access to a listing service and then post your property for sale, the sale of a business is considerably more complex and has many, many more opportunities for problems and challenges. For example, in the sale of real estate, you want it to be known to as many people as possible that your property is for sale so that you can maximize your odds of finding the right buyer. In the case of the sale of your company, however, this is in most cases exactly the wrong strategy.

Ideally, you would be able to make one phone call to exactly the right buyer and close the deal. This is obviously unrealistic, but in the case of a sale of a company, you have to be concerned about confidentiality and about the potential disruption to your business when too many people come to know your company is for sale. In sum, selling your business requires delicate handling, which is why we highly recommend hiring an advisor or team of advisors experienced in managing confidential transactions.

A Second Note of Caution: Understand the Risks of Going to Market. When you take your business to market, you need to be aware of the different risks this entails. First, understand that when you decide to go to market, notwithstanding all the protections you and your advisors put in place for confidentiality, in our experience there is a greater than even chance that at some point during the process it will become known to at least one of your employees, customers, suppliers, partners, or other business relations. We discuss how to deal with this risk in detail in subsequent chapters.

There is also a risk your business will not be sold, which can be devastating to some of your key employees if they have been involved in the process, and might even cause them to look elsewhere for new employment if they feel your company is somehow in trouble because a transaction did not close. Each of these risks is manageable, but it is important to be aware of them and prepare for them well in advance.

To mitigate these risks, work with your advisors and seek advice on how to best handle these situations. With proper planning and preparation, the sale process can be managed like any other business process with efficiency and effectiveness.

CHAPTER 9

ADVISORS: ARE THEY WORTH THE MONEY?

I n our experience, most successful entrepreneurs are religious about one of the cardinal rules of a successful business: control your expenses. As a result, many of these entrepreneurs have an allergic reaction to paying accountants, lawyers, transaction advisors, or investment bankers for services related to the sale of their business because it is hard for them to understand the value these parties bring to the table. We have been on both sides. We have been business owners and managers having to make this same decision, and we have been advisors trying to convince a business owner of the value of our services. In short, selling or buying a company is a business process like many other processes, but it is complex, and when poorly managed can be very expensive and disruptive, not only in financial terms but in business and emotional terms as well.

For most business owners their business is their primary asset. Therefore, our general advice is that hiring an expert when it comes to the process of buying or selling a business is usually a good investment because an advisor can help you avoid the expensive mistakes that can often occur during the course of a transaction. When done skillfully, an advisor's participation can enhance the value you receive for your business.

Hiring a Transaction Advisor or Investment Banker. When hiring an advisor to help you sell or buy a business, it is important that you thoroughly review their expertise, experience, references, and credentials. Moreover, you need to be comfortable with them as individuals. Don't settle necessarily on the first advisor you meet – take your time and evaluate multiple advisors. The best advisors are very comfortable competing for your business. In addition, while price is important, make sure you understand what your advisor is promising to deliver, and evaluate those promises skeptically.

For example, we have had clients who interviewed with other advisors who promised to have their business sold at a high valuation "in two months." Having managed dozens of transactions, we can tell you that selling a business in two months is definitely a stretch. You are relying on your advisor for candid feedback and objective assessments. The first test of this candor and objectivity should come in how they review the sale process with you. Don't be misled by false promises, and be sure you are not making a decision based on someone telling you what you want to hear. You need your advisor to be objective, factual, and to exercise good judgment. You do not want your advisor to simply tell you your business is worth more than it is and that a sale will be easy.

In a sale, your advisor will be representing your business, so you need to be confident they can do it well. As part of our Seller's ToolKit (which we will gladly provide upon request), we include a sample Request for Proposal ("RFP") that you can use with potential advisors that asks a number of important questions. Any advisor worth hiring will be willing to answer these questions in writing. Your research should not stop with the RFP, however. We also recommend that you speak with an advisor's prior clients and that you spend enough time with an advisor to get comfortable with them personally.

In addition, when speaking with a potential advisor, how detailed are they in asking questions about your business? Do you get the sense they understand your industry and company well enough to properly represent you in the market? Only you will be able to answer these questions, but make sure you spend enough time and effort during this phase of the project to make a solid decision. Otherwise, you risk having to go through the entire process again in 6-18 months when your relationship with a specific advisor does not work out. We have had more than a few clients who previously engaged with another advisor that did not work out. It is not pleasant for any of the parties involved and it makes the second attempt at selling even more difficult.

<u>Why Hire An Advisor?</u> An advisor does several things for you. First and foremost, an advisor should be able to do a comprehensive review of your business and estimate its value based on a number of different methodologies, as we discussed earlier. There are certainly business brokers and advisors who will run a cursory "rule of thumb" assessment or estimate of your business to arrive at a value. However, remember that the valuation you get can only be as good as the underlying research and market data reviewed. The old adage is true here – you get what you pay for.

Given the critical importance of the valuation of your company in relation to your post-closing financial needs, we highly recommend getting as thorough a valuation as you can afford so that you understand not only what your company is worth, but also how a transaction is likely to be structured and what factors impact your company's value, positively or negatively. A solid valuation will also include market data gleaned from a variety of available databases that will give you some context of what happened in other similar transactions in your industry. Be careful of a "quick" or "rule of thumb" valuation from your advisor – in certain cases, advisors will tell you what you want to hear in order to earn your business, which can be very damaging in the long run. Remember, you want an objective assessment of your business from which you will make life-changing decisions. Making these important decisions on incorrect or incomplete information will only cause trouble later.

Second, a qualified and experienced advisor or investment banker will be able to insulate you from the day-to-day activities of the deal process. These can include preparing information about your company to deliver to prospective buyers, preparing the list of qualified bidders to contact, making daily calls to likely buyers, qualifying buyers, handling questions about your business, negotiating confidentiality agreements, and helping manage due diligence and the negotiation of letters of intent. These are all activities that could significantly distract you from your principal occupation of operating your business. In addition, attempting to navigate and negotiate each of these issues without a lot of experience will likely result in a lower value for your company than you would otherwise be able to obtain with a quality advisor. A qualified advisor can take all these issues off your plate and allow you to focus on your business. Selling a business is not like selling a house – it is considerably more complex and carries with it significantly more risk.

Finding an Advisor. Probably the best place to find candidates to be your transaction advisor or investment bank are referrals from your attorney, accountant, or financial advisor. These professionals will likely have worked with a firm in the past that their prior clients feel positively about. These professionals have a vested interest in making sure they recommend only qualified advisors, as it would reflect poorly on them otherwise. Ask a couple of your key advisors for a few names, and soon you will have a solid list of quality transaction advisors from which to choose.

Whom to Hire? We have a bias in favor of advisors who have both a transactional background and an operating background. Even better, if you can find an advisor who has operated a business either in the process of or following an acquisition, they will bring special experience and wisdom, which will be of significant value to you. The reason for this is simple: advisors who have walked in your shoes and who know how business really operates will be better able to understand your business, and therefore better able to represent your business in the market. Moreover, they will be able to help you add value to your business before and during a transaction with objective suggestions based on experience. Advisors who have no operating experience typically do not share this level of insight into how your business is operated or how it can be improved. Similarly, if an advisor has not had to manage employees, customers, and vendors during a sale process, they will likely not be as able to advise you on critical communication issues when the need arises (and it will arise).

A qualified advisor or investment banker should be able to earn their fees by getting several bidders to the table in a controlled environment (what is sometimes referred to as a "soft auction" or "controlled auction"), and getting each bidder to make their best offer. We have used this technique in every deal we have managed and find it works exceedingly well. We don't negotiate with just one buyer, and in reality, we don't really negotiate at all. We simply make buyers aware that there are other bidders in the process, and that they will be best served by putting their best foot forward. Some buyers do not like being in a competitive bidding environment, which is certainly understandable, but such buyers typically will not pay a premium for your business anyway. Unless a buyer has a sterling reputation for enhancing value so that your business will be able to make even more money after a sale (if Warren Buffett were to buy your company, for example), we typically advise sellers to bring as many qualified parties to the table as is manageable. In most cases, this will be three to five parties.

A few caveats about hiring an advisor or investment banker: in addition to the questions highlighted by the RFP included in our Seller's ToolKit, you should make sure that the firm or individual you hire has successfully sold businesses in the past and, indeed, that a substantial majority of the businesses he or she takes to market are in fact sold. There are a few firms in the market today who employ high-pressure sales tactics during seminars, take a substantial fee up front, but then rely simply on mailers to their generic buyer database to sell their clients, only to see businesses languish on the market for two or three years or more. These firms will often have punitive cancellation provisions and rely in large part on their up-front fees to earn their revenues versus a success-based fee which is paid when you receive your sale proceeds. We much prefer to see an arrangement with advisors where the majority of fees are based on a successful transaction so that your interests and the advisor's interests are in perfect alignment. In any case, it is critical to understand how your fees are determined.

Fees. The fees that your advisor will charge you will vary significantly from firm to firm, and will depend on transaction size and complexity. There are several different structures, ranging from a "reverse Lehman" formula, which pays a declining percentage of each successive million dollars. In smaller transactions, this might be 10% of the first million, 8% of the second million, 6% of the third million, and 4% of each dollar thereafter, or in larger deals this might be reduced to 5%/4%/3%/2%/1%. Fees can also be a flat fee, or simply a fixed percentage. For example, in a $10 million transaction, the fee might be $520,000 as shown below:

> ➢ 10% of the first $1 million, or $100,000, <u>plus</u>
> ➢ 8% of the second $1 million, or $80,000, <u>plus</u>
> ➢ 6% of the third $1 million, or $60,000, <u>plus</u>
> ➢ 4% of the remaining consideration ($7 million), or $280,000
> ➢ For a total of $520,000, or 5.2% of the total transaction value.

Each deal is unique, so it is hard to assess what structures your banker might propose, but ultimately you need to assess the value your advisor is adding to assess whether the fees they charge are reasonable. When checking references, be sure to ask whether the seller feels they received adequate value for the fees they paid. If your advisor has done a solid job understanding and positioning your business, has found several solid buyers, has helped negotiate a good transaction at maximum value, and has helped you navigate many of the pitfalls which accompany a sale transaction, he will have more than paid for his fees.

<u>Engage Your Advisors Early</u>. Just like tax planners, we like to get involved with our clients early enough that we know we can have a positive impact on value. If we are engaged by a client just prior to when they are ready to go to market, our ability to help that client improve the value of their business is limited. Conversely, if we are able to get involved with a client six months or more ahead of when they anticipate going to market and we can help identify and evaluate the different Value Drivers within their business, we are then able to work with them to improve their business and increase its value to potential buyers.

Engaging your advisor early also allows you to spend enough quality time to truly develop a comprehensive, well considered plan to go to market. This plan will include not only a valuation and the steps to go to market, but will also include a communication plan so that you as the business owner are prepared to handle any critical issues that may arise during the sale process. Having this plan and a clear set of objectives also makes the process less stressful and emotional, all of which we have found helps facilitate a good transaction experience.

The All-Important First Interview. One of the first steps your advisor or investment banker should take is to interview you extensively about your business. We spend a significant amount of time conducting due diligence on our clients so that we can learn their business and industry inside and out. This due diligence involves interviews with our client, as well as a review of their financials and key documents including specific contracts, marketing and business plans, as well as other corporate documents. This is critical for a number of different reasons: first, we need to understand their business to determine a realistic assessment of value and probable transaction structure; second, it helps us best position the business in the market to maximize value; third, we can better anticipate the inevitable buyer objections and develop strategies to address these up front; and finally, it helps us keep the seller out of the daily grind of the deal while the company is in the market by being able to answer questions that otherwise would require the seller's input.

Communicating with Your Advisor. As calls to buyers are made by your advisor, you should get periodic updates to understand what response your company is getting in the market. This is important for a number of different reasons, the most important of which is that it gives you a framework or context in which to evaluate potential offers. We like to share the example of one of our clients who worked with an unnamed competitor of ours and over a period of 18 months talked with this advisor only two or three times, and during that period received one offer. He was of course strongly encouraged to take the offer because it was a "great deal." Our client was obviously very anxious about the offer as he had no context in which to evaluate it because the advisor spent no time explaining what he was hearing in the market, the potential bidders with whom he talked, or how the market was reacting to our client's company. The client ultimately decided to pass on that offer and then hired our firm market his business. We were successful in finding a better deal for him with better terms, in a short period of time. More importantly, because we kept him informed about our progress each week, he knew how many potential bidders we approached, what their responses were, and the different offers we generated for his company. Armed with all of this information, he was able to make a much better decision about which offer to take when the time came to sign a letter of intent.

The point, however, is this: you must receive timely communication from which you can make a logical and unemotional decision regarding the sale of your company. If you have to demand information from an advisor in terms of updates, you may find yourself frustrated and lacking confidence in whether or not your transaction may get done. If you talk with your advisor weekly or bi-weekly, make sure you get progress reports (we prefer to use written reports with our clients), so you will be fully informed during the entire process. You will know how many potential buyers your advisor has contacted, what their responses have been, and the general interest level in your business.

If your advisor targets 300 potential bidders and 295 of them decline for various reasons that the advisor can summarize for you (for example, too small, too big, or too far outside a bidder's competency), but five come forward with offers of different types that can be compared to one another, you will now be able to make a much more informed decision about the ultimate offer you decide to accept or reject.

CHAPTER 10

Once your advisor has learned your business in detail, he will typically prepare two versions of a "book" that describes your business. The first version, what we refer to as a "teaser" document, is a one- or two-page "generic" description of your company. The objective of this "teaser" document is to provide enough information to get a potential bidder interested in learning more, but not enough information that someone could figure out that your particular business is for sale.

The second version of the book is a much more comprehensive description of your company that is only provided to potential bidders once they have been screened and have signed a confidentiality or non-disclosure agreement (forms of which are available from your attorney or our Seller's ToolKit). This second version should include detailed financials and forecasts, an overall description of your market, your operations, assets, customers, employee base, marketing plans, management biographies, and other details that a potential bidder would need to see to formulate an indication of interest in your business. Again, it is worth your time to review these versions of the "book" as this will be the first impression of your business in the market and should be compelling enough to generate further interest.

The Best Books. When interviewing advisors, be sure to ask for copies of past books they have prepared for previous clients (redacted to protect confidentiality, of course). Read through the books. Are they thoroughly detailed, or are they generic descriptions of the business? Does the book present the business in a uniquely persuasive fashion, focused on the key selling points of the business, or is it hard to see why the business would be a compelling purchase for a potential buyer? Does the book give you as the reader a good picture of the business and the key operating metrics? Does the book look professional, or is it simply tax returns stapled together with some brief verbiage to go in front? Does the book position the company in the current market at the time it was written? Does the book sound too much like a sales pitch?

Once you see a high-quality, detailed book, you will immediately notice a difference from lesser-quality, generic presentations. There is a balance, of course, between giving the reader so much information that they get lost in the details and giving the reader so little information that they are not sure what the business really does or how it works. The real test for a book is whether it can give an accurate description of the business so that buyers understand the big picture, but leave a reader with the desire to learn more. Remember, this book is the tool to get buyers to look deeper, which means it must be interesting and inspire them to ask the next set of questions.

The topics your book should cover include: a general overview of the business and its market, including what makes it unique in the market; a review of marketing and sales; a discussion of operations; an organization chart and discussion of the management team; a summary of your competition and how you are positioned in the market; a discussion of your major customers and major suppliers and the length and character of your relationships with each; and a financial presentation which includes your income statement and balance sheet and a discussion of important trends.

Presentation of Your Business. Every successful business has a unique set of strengths that will be of interest to potential buyers. These strengths could include an exclusive product, service offering or territory, a distinguished customer base, a great set of processes consistently executed, a talented and mature management team, or any one of a number of other factors. The best advisors will be able to draw these strengths out, present them in a clear and convincing fashion, and use these differentiating characteristics to enhance the ultimate value of a transaction for you. In selecting an advisor, you will want to make sure your advisor either does or has the capacity to understand your business in detail at an operational level. This type of expertise typically comes from years of experience in the business world, acting in a variety of capacities, not just as an advisor.

On occasion, particularly when dealing with a niche company that might be attractive to different types of strategic buyers for different reasons, we have drafted multiple versions of the same book. In each different version, we might choose to highlight different aspects of our client's business based on what we think will be of most interest to buyers in a specific industry segment. Again, the goal is to generate interest in your company and to provide buyers with a logical argument for why they would benefit from owning your company. Often these reasons are different from buyer to buyer, and your advisor's job through his conversations with each buyer is to uncover why a specific buyer is interested in your company and leverage that in future negotiations.

The best advisors, in our opinion, are those who have been in the business world, understand the challenges and nuances of operating successful businesses, and based on their experience have a keen understanding of business in general. You can tell a lot about the quality of an advisor by listening to the depth and breadth of the questions they ask you. Too many advisors spend their interview time with you telling you all about themselves. Be sure you pick an advisor who asks a lot of questions, and more importantly, listens to your answers. Advisors who listen well are then be able to present your business favorably and will be able to give you the best advice. This expertise and ability to understand your business also means they should be able to understand your industry and its unique value chain, which will in turn help them to identify the best and most comprehensive list of potential bidders.

CHAPTER 11

SOURCING BUYERS & TYPES OF BUYERS

G oing to Market – What to Avoid. Once your book has been prepared in its different versions, advisors have different strategies for how they will go to market. Again, our view is biased given our experience, approach, and success, but some business brokers or advisors will take the generic description of your business and add it to the list of their other clients and distribute that to their mailing lists, or they might post it on their website or other websites that advertise businesses for sale (for example, www.bizbuysell.com, or www.mergernetwork.com). We are not fans of this approach for a number of different reasons.

First, posting your business description, however generic, on a website or indiscriminately broadcasting it in e-mails or letters significantly increases the risk that someone who should not be privy to such information will find out your business is for sale, compromising confidentiality. This will cause major headaches for you with employees, suppliers, customers, and competitors.

Second, soliciting interest in this "shotgun approach" is likely to generate a lot of "window shoppers" who either may not be qualified or may not be truly interested in completing an acquisition, or who might be competitors interested in simply learning more about your business. At best, this will result in wasted time on your part as you and your advisors try to sort through all the different bidders. At worst, it gives your competitors information, however generic, about your business, including the possibility that they find out your company is for sale and/or start a rumor in the industry.

Neither of these consequences is good, so we don't advocate this approach. We compare these approaches to eBay: buyers using eBay

97

are not intending to pay top dollar for their purchases; similarly, you do not want to deal with a bunch of potentially unqualified bidders who are simply bargain-shopping. It will waste your time and frustrate you, with a low probability for success.

Targeting Buyers. A much better approach, in our opinion, is a targeted or "rifle shot" research process to identify a list of likely candidates, whether financial (private equity firms, for example) or strategic (firms that work along the value chain of your company). This approach requires a lot of effort, to be sure, but we have found that it minimizes the possibility of window-shopping by unqualified or uninterested parties because we first fully vet the list. It also dramatically reduces the potential for an inadvertent disclosure of the fact that our client's business is for sale because we contact only specific parties that our clients have approved.

In addition, rather than sending out a list of multiple companies for sale, where it is challenging to differentiate one firm from another, the best process relies on directed calling to C-level decision makers (CEO's, COO's, or CFO's). Again, we are all products of our own experiences, but having been a buyer, seller, and advisor on dozens of transactions, we believe this approach, while time-consuming and laborious, is the best one we have found to ensure the best possible offers from the most qualified buyers.

Process for Buyer Identification. This targeted approach also requires that your advisor have a well-defined process for identifying and contacting prospective bidders to maximize the potential of reaching solid buyer candidates who are likely to make an offer or have interest in your company. This process should include a sign-off by you as the owner because there may be potential bidders that are competitors or that you would not want to be contacted for some other reason.

As you review the list of potential bidders your advisor wants to contact, pay attention not only to potential competitors, but also suppliers and customers to make sure you don't inadvertently put an important relationship at risk. You may still elect to have your advisor call some of these parties, but you might have them position the call a little differently or you may want to reach out directly to those parties ahead of time to provide them with appropriate context.

Your advisor should also schedule a regular call or meeting with you to review progress, reporting back to you what common themes he is hearing in the market, what parties have expressed initial interest, and how his initial market assessment is being validated or not. This constant communication with you will give you important context, creating a background against which you will be able to make more informed decisions when the time comes to evaluate offers. In our experience, this type of communication gives clients a running storyline on their company's potential in the market, so when they receive an offer (or offers, hopefully) for their business, they already understand roughly where the market is and how they should view the offer(s). Without this context, an owner is unlikely to feel very confident about whether to sell, make a counter-offer, or reject the proposal altogether. So, as you interview potential advisors, make sure you thoroughly explore their plans for communication with you and with prospective buyers.

Contacting Potential Bidders. Once the book is complete, and a list of potential bidders has been prepared that you have approved in advance, the next step is to reach out to potential bidders to determine their interest level. As we discussed above, the best strategy is not to advertise your business in mass e-mailings, or to post your business on the Internet, or to include your business in a standard mailing of a firm's listings. These approaches substantially raise the risk of a breach of confidentiality and frankly do very little to target the best buyers for your business. Many buyers will ignore these mass mailings because the listings are for the most part the same month after month, and businesses that linger on these lists will be at risk of being labeled "damaged goods".

The better approach is to direct the solicitation effort toward those potential bidders to whom your business could be strategically important. This includes industry buyers as well as financial buyers who may already have an investment in your space and are looking to build their portfolio companies through acquisitions, which is a common strategy among private equity firms. Our recommended approach is to reach out directly to the decision makers – CEOs, COO's, CFOs, Managing Directors or Partners. Just as in your typical sales call, you will save a lot of time and headache by going directly to the decision maker because he or she can tell you immediately whether such an acquisition is of interest and can make the process run a lot more efficiently. There are several potential buyers your advisor may reach out to, and as a seller, you should understand how these buyers behave and operate and why they might be good or bad for your specific business.

Strategic Buyers. As we have discussed, sophisticated buyers place a premium on predictability of earnings. Yet, there are also buyers who may have other reasons to purchase a specific business that are not immediately apparent. For example, some companies may purchase other companies because they want to jump-start operations in a particular geography, or they have a specific product gap that an acquired company could fill. In these cases, a buyer may have its own way of determining value that is different from standard financial analysis. Even in these cases, however, the purchase must ultimately be justified by the eventual return on investment generated by the acquisition, in whatever way this may be determined. A strategic buyer will only be willing to pay so much – typically up to the point at which they feel they could replicate the existing business in the absence of an acquisition, or the price they are able to pay for a similar company in the market.

As a result, when we have sellers who are in markets where there is significant strategic interest, we spend a lot of time and energy trying to understand the underlying strategic intent of the potential buyers so that we can leverage that interest to the maximum extent possible in our positioning of the company in the market and in negotiations. Ultimately, if you as the seller are able to position your company in the best light possible for the specific buyer you are targeting, you will maximize the value of your company.

Strategic buyers can take many forms and can come from many

different places along the value chain. Make sure your advisors have a detailed, documented process for uncovering where these buyers might be. In our experience, they are rarely in an advisor's generic database.

Financial Buyers. The other category of professional buyer is what we refer to as "financial" buyers. Financial buyers are professional investors who typically have a fund available to invest or who may have a set of investors who have agreed to finance certain types of transactions. These financial buyers are private equity funds, venture capital funds, buyout funds, search funds, and private investment funds. Their focus is typically on buying low and selling high, but they are often expert at structuring attractive deals that can be a win/win for both buyer and seller.

Financial buyers are usually very sophisticated, have a ready pool of money available to invest, and can run a transaction very well, which is often attractive to sellers. Financial buyers can also be strategic in nature, such as when they already have a portfolio business in the same or related industry and are looking to build their existing portfolio company through acquisition.

Alternatively, financial buyers might be strategic insofar as they are looking for the right "platform" acquisition from which they can build a larger entity through other acquisitions. Financial buyers also offer sellers the opportunity at a "second bite at the apple." For example, a financial buyer might want to purchase only 60% of a company, with the seller retaining the remaining 40%, which can then be sold at a later date, hopefully at a higher price as the business grows and continues to prosper. This "second bite" is particularly attractive in situations where historically a seller's growth has been limited because of a lack of available capital (which the financial buyer can hopefully provide). In all cases, if you are considering accepting a letter of intent from a financial buyer, you should insist on speaking with other business owners (both current and former) who have worked with that buyer so that you can understand what life will be like following acquisition.

The Entrepreneurial Buyer. Similarly, there are thousands of ex-executives who elect to go into business for themselves, and have decided that acquiring a business is the fastest and most effective way for them to make a living while working for themselves. These professionals may be in the business because they want to do something on their own, or because they are looking for a specific lifestyle that operating a business can support. We don't want to categorically disparage these buyers, because there are plenty of solid, reputable buyers like this in the market.

However, we generally advise clients to be cautious because these buyers often struggle to obtain solid financing and they typically do not have a lot of experience conducting acquisitions. These factors can slow the overall process of the transaction considerably and in our experience, time kills deals. However, these buyers, particularly with smaller transactions that they can finance with Small Business Administration loans for generally less than $1 million, are sometimes willing to pay more for a specific company because they have reasons to complete an acquisition outside of the financial prospects of the acquired company.

Search Funds. In the past ten to twenty years, search funds have emerged as an interesting category of business buyer. Search funds are typically funded by a group of high net-worth investors who initially invest a modest amount to finance an individual or small group of individuals who are looking to purchase a business. The initial investment is to fund the search process, and once an acquisition candidate is approved, the initial investors have the option to invest in the subsequent acquisition. Many search funds are raised by recent business school graduates who are interested in running their own business, and the business schools at Stanford and Harvard have been strong advocates for this type of investment. The sponsored individual or team of individuals is interested in managing the business after closing, which can be an attractive solution for business owners who are looking to exit daily operations after a sale. From a seller's perspective, the critical issues to consider are: the quality and credibility of the individuals who would be running your company following the sale, the depth of their financing capacity, and their seriousness about acquiring your company.

Competitors. Although we are typically very cautious when approaching a client's competitors as potential buyers, they can often be a perfect candidate if they are handled with extreme care. Competitors see value not only in the future cash flows of the acquired company; they may also be able to enjoy a better position in the market. Moreover, competitors may be able to leverage their existing infrastructure to reduce overall administrative costs of the combined entity, allowing them to pay a premium for an acquisition over fair market value. We typically like to approach competitors only late in the sale process, after we have had a chance to test the rest of the market, primarily because going to a competitor has risks that are more real and significant than with other potential buyers. For example, if a sale is explored but ultimately does not occur, a competitor now has information about your company that could be very detrimental to your ongoing operations if used inappropriately. Moreover, although everyone reviewing your company and its records should be bound by a signed confidentiality agreement, it is no secret that on occasion leaks occur. This could be very challenging for your company if word of an acquisition leaked to your employees, customers, or suppliers. As a result, we typically recommend going to competitors only after other alternatives have been explored first.

In short, the process for identifying, soliciting, and generating interest from potential bidders, just as with the parts of the go-to-market process, needs to be carefully planned, executed with discipline, and communicated frequently to you as the client. This part of the process is the riskiest in terms of potential confidentiality breaches, so make sure it is appropriately discriminating and well managed by professionals who have done it before.

CHAPTER 12

LETTERS OF INTENT, DUE DILIGENCE, AND LAWYERS

The Letter of Intent. Once your advisor has generated indications of interest from buyers, your advisor will request letters of intent, which are non-binding descriptions of what a potential buyer is willing to pay for your business and how the buyer intends to structure a transaction. You will then need to decide which offer is likely to be the best one for you. This can be a complicated process, but your advisor should be able to help you navigate the different offers in a logical, organized fashion. We like to compare each of the offers side-by-side for our clients, which we have found is a good way for clients to see and weigh all the issues. In comparing offers, you will want to look at a number of different factors, including:

- ➢ What is the overall offer price or total valuation of the company?

- ➢ Method of payment – for example, how much is in cash up front, and how much is in seller notes or stock and how will the buyer provide subsequent liquidity for any of these non-cash components?

- ➢ What is the legal structure of the acquisition? For example, is it a purchase of stock or assets, and what does this mean to you in terms of taxes?

- ➢ Is there a minimum level of working capital (current assets less current liabilities) required to be left in the business at closing, and if so, what is it and how will that impact overall valuation?

- ➢ Is there a period of time during which you commit to dealing exclusively with this particular buyer, and if so, is that period reasonable?

➢ What are the employment or consulting contract terms and payments?

➢ What is the likely ability of the company to close the transaction? For example, do they need to locate financing first, or do they have their financing already lined up?

➢ What is the quality of the acquiring management team or private equity firm? What kind of people are they and what value system do they adhere to?

➢ What is the anticipated time to closing? This is where experienced buyers can look more attractive than inexperienced buyers because they have a pre-existing process for closing a transaction that can often shorten the time to closing and can also reduce the risk of different issues disrupting the process because they are experienced at resolving and handling such issues. Don't underestimate the importance of the speed and efficiency of getting to the closing. We know many business owners who have wasted time, money, and energy with inexperienced buyers only to regret it later.

➢ Are the assumptions underlying valuation clear and understandable? Make sure your advisor dives into this with potential buyers because the last thing you want is to sign a letter of intent, go through due diligence and contract negotiations, only to find that the buyer was under a completely different set of assumptions about your business and is not willing to pay what they promised.

➢ What is the prior acquisition history of the buyer? Similar to dealing with experienced buyers, it is also helpful to understand what type of buyers you are dealing with. For example, although a small minority of buyers, there are some that we refer to as "bait and switch" buyers – they will promise you a really solid offer up front, but during due diligence, which can be protracted and expensive, their offer deteriorates and they use the pressure on you to sell to leverage themselves into a better contract price and terms. Don't underestimate the psychological investment you will make in the sale process – these buyers understand this type of commitment very well and use it to their advantage. Avoid these buyers if at all possible because they will only disappoint you and waste your money and time. On the other hand, most buyers do deal in good faith and are generally easy to work with as you handle the different issues that arise during due diligence and contract negotiations. Again, your advisor can help you do your own due diligence on potential bidders so you can truly understand with whom you are dealing.

There are certainly other factors to consider when comparing different offers, but these cover most of the major issues. In our experience, all of the issues other than total valuation can be at least as or more important than the overall dollar value. Remember, the total deal value is only relevant if you actually receive all of that value. If it is contingent on other factors or may deteriorate during due diligence, then it really is not the same offer, so pay attention to these other factors when doing your own evaluation.

If there are issues that concern you during the letter of intent negotiations, make sure to address them head on rather than waiting to address them during contract negotiations. If you can address issues early, particularly during the letter of intent negotiations, your odds of resolving them are much greater, and if it is truly a deal breaker for you or the buyer, then you will have saved yourself a lot of time.

Legal Review. Once you have decided on a particular offer letter or letter of intent, you should have your attorney review it to make sure you understand any legal commitments contained in it, and whether there are any specific legal issues of which you should be aware. The clauses you should pay particular attention to are ones that relate to exclusivity (the time period during which you cannot solicit interest from other bidders – buyers request this in exchange for the time and money they will be investing in due diligence), anything that relates to termination fees (fees that a seller might have to pay if they back out of a transaction – these are typically rare in smaller deals, but we have seen them proposed), and of course the material deal terms (an experienced deal attorney can help you understand these and ensure that they are consistent with your understanding of the transaction in general).

Due Diligence. Once you have executed the offer letter, indication of interest, or letter of intent (different buyers use different terms), the process of due diligence and contract documentation begins. Typically, a buyer will have a standard due diligence checklist (we have included an example of one in Appendix B), which will request that you produce corporate records, contracts, financials, legal information, and other types of information.

We generally recommend to our clients that they prepare due diligence materials well in advance. While some of the items on the standard list will change over time (such as financial information), there are many items (contracts and other corporate documents) that you can prepare, copy, and organize well before due diligence begins. As we have said before, time kills deals, so the shorter the period between signing the letter of intent and closing, the better. In order to make sure the due diligence process is completed as efficiently as possible, you should have your due diligence information prepared and ready to go as soon as possible after the letter of intent is signed.

To do this, we suggest that sellers prepare their due diligence prior to signing their letter of intent. This accomplishes three key objectives: first, it reduces the time to closing because the process does not have to wait until you get your information prepared. Second, it presents a solid, well-organized first impression to the buyer, the power of which cannot be underestimated. Finally, if for some reason your legal or other information is incomplete or your advisors determine there are issues with your information, you can resolve these issues ahead of time. We recommend to our clients that they prepare the information in two sets: the first set they keep as a copy of what has been presented to the buyer, and the second set is for the buyer (who should return the materials if the transaction does not proceed). This way, if the current transaction breaks down and you have to go through the process with another bidder, you will have your information already prepared. Your attorney can also help manage this process, although be mindful of the legal fees incurred to prepare this information.

As a general piece of advice, be as transparent and objective as possible in your due diligence materials and in answering questions. Hopefully you and your advisors will have already discussed the potential issues and weaknesses in your company and addressed them ahead of time so that due diligence does not present the buyer with any big surprises. Nevertheless, where there is an issue, deal with it promptly and candidly. Buyers understand that every business has challenges, but good buyers will not look favorably on a seller or future manager of theirs being disingenuous with them. Also, involve your key managers (your financial officer in particular), because they will be accountable for collecting and disseminating a large amount of information and you need to keep them focused on the task at hand.

Due diligence is perhaps the most challenging part of the process for many sellers because it can take time, it involves sometimes difficult discussions about the seller's business, and can sometimes decrease the value of the transaction to the seller when the buyer finds different issues or problems with the business. In addition, during due diligence a seller will often think he has provided all of the information a buyer should require, but we have to remind our clients that buyers do not know the business as well as an owner does, which means they will look at the business differently and will often want to see information presented in a different way than the company compiles it. This is often the case with financial information as a buyer tries to understand different types of revenue sources, different clients, different suppliers, and different types of expenses.

Many sellers have tailored their financial statements over time to meet their particular needs and they are sometimes not as precise as

buyers would like to see, which can create additional work for a seller if they are required to create different types of reports or summaries. At the extreme, this can be incredibly frustrating and taxing for
a seller, but your advisor should help moderate the buyer's requests.
At times, your advisor may need to step in to be the "bad cop" by
pushing back when the information requests become excessive.

In addition to having to prepare information in different formats,
buyers will also ask a lot of questions in their attempt to better understand the business. This is very normal, but can be tedious for sellers. As an advisor, we try to "batch process" buyers' questions for
our clients so that they are not constantly being hounded by buyers
with questions, but even under the best processes, good buyers ask a
lot of questions. We try to help our clients put themselves in the position of a buyer so that they comprehend what the buyer is trying to
understand. In some cases, the buyer is simply trying to understand
the business better, and in other cases, they are building a case for a
lower valuation. Be on the lookout for the latter motivation and try to
short-circuit these discussions as soon as possible.

As a transaction drags on, a seller can lose valuable negotiating
leverage. This is true for a number of reasons – the seller becomes
psychologically invested in the deal, the seller's employees may become aware of the transaction (and the failure of the transaction can
cause them distress and disrupt the business), or the seller may have
already started to mentally spend the money he expects to receive
from the deal. As a result, the goal for the seller and his advisors is to
shorten the time to closing as much as possible by being prepared,
responsive, and having an advisor to push the process with the buyer
and each side's attorneys.

During due diligence, the buyer typically will prepare acquisition
contracts. These can include the asset or stock purchase agreement
(which is the primary purchase contract and should generally mirror
the terms included in the letter of intent), an employment or consulting contract, non-compete agreements (which are typically part of
the purchase contract and employment or consulting contract), buy-
sell arrangements where the buyer and seller agree on how to dispose

of each party's shares in the future, and other agreements. Your attorney should be able to familiarize you with these documents and their importance.

Buyer Due Diligence. As important as the buyer's due diligence is on your company, you will want to conduct due diligence on potential buyers, particularly if you intend to sign a letter of intent with one of them. Your advisor may have already completed some preliminary financial due diligence on the potential bidders to ensure they have adequate financial resources to consummate a transaction. In addition, your advisor may ask for references from prior sellers with whom the buyer has completed transactions. You as the seller may meet personally with the buyer to ask them questions about their overall management philosophies, their timeline and plan for the due diligence process, their strategy for the business going forward, how they plan to integrate the business (if at all) with their existing business(es), and other questions that will help you as the seller understand cultural fit, the ability for the buyer to complete the transaction, and what to expect after closing.

Contracts. Once the buyer presents the first draft of the acquisition documents, you, your transaction advisor, and your attorney will want to get together and review them. You should pay particular attention to the material deal terms, including any lingering indemnity obligations (your agreement to handle liabilities that occur after closing), representations and warranties you are expected to make (these are statements by you about the condition of your company that the buyer is relying on and can use to sue you later if they turn out to be false), and other terms your attorney will alert you to.

Use your attorney to help you evaluate the materiality or significance of the different issues in your purchase agreement and other contracts. Although not in the scope of this book, the key issues will include representations and warranties, indemnities, conditions precedent to closing, caps on liabilities, baskets, covenants not to compete, and terms of employment or consulting contracts. Each of these can be a material issue to you personally, so be sure to discuss the importance of these with your attorney and investment banker so they can help balance these to maximize the value of the deal to you.

Many sellers have attorneys they have worked with for years on their corporate matters or litigation matters, and as such, prefer to use these same attorneys to handle their sale transaction. While this may make sense because you trust your corporate attorney and he knows your business, in our experience it is far better to hire a transaction attorney or an attorney who specializes in handling mergers and acquisitions. Having a specialist who handles transactions day in and day out ensures that you are hiring someone who will work efficiently and who will understand quickly what issues are worth fighting over and what issues are unimportant. If the attorneys start arguing over minor points and ignore the important ones, your legal bills go up, the time to closing is extended, your relationship with the buyer will become strained, and the probability of closing deteriorates. For these reasons, make sure you hire an attorney who understands the process and can efficiently and cost-effectively represent you.

As an example of how expensive it is to have an inexperienced attorney handle a transaction, we had a client whose financials were deteriorating and whose attorney took four weeks to turn around his comments on a fairly standard set of acquisition documents. During this four week period, which in our opinion should have taken three to four days at most, our client's financials deteriorated to such an extent that the overall valuation for the business went down by over a half million dollars. Needless to say, the attorney's bill paled in comparison to the overall reduction in value of the deal. The lesson here is to hire the expert when picking your attorney – it will pay off. Your transaction advisor can also refer you to experienced deal attorneys they have worked with in the past, and your corporate attorney may also have members in his or her firm who specialize in transactions.

Depending on the structure of the transaction, the buyer will either buy your assets (equipment, vehicles, furniture, goodwill, etc.) or your stock (the shares of ownership in your company). One of the important elements of either type of transaction is what is typically referred to as a "Schedule of Exceptions." As we discussed above, you will be asked to make various representations and warranties about your company in the stock or asset purchase agreement. In the Schedule of Exceptions, you will have the opportunity to make exceptions to the representations and warranties you are making.

For example, the purchase agreement might include a boilerplate representation that you have no current litigation pending. If you currently are involved in litigation, this representation would get you into trouble unless you included in your Schedule of Exceptions a reference to and description of the current pending litigation. Ideally, anything you decide to include in the Schedule of Exceptions would already have been included in the materials you provided to the buyer during due diligence. Otherwise, when you list something the buyer is not familiar with, it will create anxiety for the buyer during a point in the process where it becomes increasingly difficult to resolve issues quickly. It is important to remember to constantly update your schedule of exceptions during the transaction process, up to and including the date of closing. Your description of the condition of your business must be accurate at the moment you sign the agreement with the buyer and at closing.

Advice on Issues. Every business has issues and defects, and we always advise clients to highlight and present potentially difficult issues with their company early – first to their advisors, who can help put the issue in context, and then to the buyer. In our experience, issues that are highlighted in the early part of due diligence can be handled more easily than when they are held back until the last part of the process. Holding issues until late in the process creates three problems: first, the buyer's level of confidence in you and the business will be significantly more adversely impacted if he believes you withheld information. If you are candid about the issue and explain its context early, the buyer will generally look favorably on this as an indication of your honesty and integrity.

Second, when issues come up early, the chances of being able to resolve them are higher because neither party will feel like they have already given up all they are going to give because of the other issues that have already been negotiated and resolved.

Third, buyer and seller are usually pretty tired by the end of the process, so introducing a significant issue late in the process makes it a lot less likely that the parties have the energy to handle it in a reasonable and effective way. As a result, talk with your attorney, accountant, and transaction advisor early on to make sure that you have presented any difficult information that might show up in the Schedule of Exceptions. This will also give you the opportunity to present the issue in the right context. In our experience, issues are seldom as bad (or as good) as they at first appear, and being able to set the right context for any issue will increase your chances of being able to resolve it and minimize the impact of it on the overall deal.

As you finalize the purchase agreements and the various schedules and wrap up due diligence, it is now time to prepare for closing the transaction. Many sellers get so focused on the closing that they neglect some important communication issues that can significantly impact how smoothly the post-closing transition goes. Having bought and sold companies and operated them afterward, we cannot stress enough how important this communication strategy is, which we discuss at length in Chapter 14.

Note of Caution: Watch Out for Pre-Closing Integration Tactics. Some buyers will be eager to start integrating your business into theirs, even ahead of closing the transaction. They will want to have employees start talking about go-forward strategies, and they may even want to talk with suppliers or maybe even customers. On occasion, they might even push you as the seller to announce the pending transaction to your employees so that the post-closing integration goes "more smoothly."

Although the buyer might have the purest intentions, be careful not to allow these pre-closing integration activities to get out of hand. We have seen more than one example where a seller told his employees about the pending transaction ahead of closing, and then had fundamental issues on the deal negotiation. Unfortunately, once you tell your employees about a transaction, you lose negotiating leverage as it becomes much more difficult and issue-plagued to then tell your employees the deal is off. Imagine their emotional roller-coaster, their perceptions about the business, and the overall level of distraction and potential damage to your business if your deal terminates. Our advice is pretty simple along these lines: prior to your sales proceeds check clearing, limit the people with knowledge about the transaction to the smallest number possible, and once the transaction is closed, you will have plenty of opportunity to explain the transaction to all the relevant constituencies (employees, customers, suppliers, partners, and others).

CHAPTER 13

DEAL STRUCTURE – MAKING OR BREAKING THE DEAL

We talked briefly about the importance of transaction structure in the context of capital structures and capital markets, and here we will handle it in a bit more depth. In short, how a transaction is structured, all the way from how payment is made to what types of ancillary agreements are involved, is a major determinant of the value of an overall transaction. However, we often find buyers and sellers are ill-informed about the nuances of deal structure, which means the smarter party will get a better deal in the end.

Transaction Structure. Transaction structures can take numerous forms, and the structure of a transaction can be as or more important than the aggregate deal value. For example, if one buyer is willing to pay $10 million for a company, and another is willing to pay $5 million for the same company, you might logically conclude the first buyer is offering a better deal. However, in the case of the first buyer, he is willing to pay $10 million, but over 20 years in $500,000 increments, assuming he continues to have the capital to do so. The second buyer is willing to pay all $5 million in cash up front. Many sellers would be much better off opting for the second buyer's offer, notwithstanding the fact that it is a lower total number, because not only is the present value of the $5 million greater than the present value of the stream of $500,000 payments (assuming a discount rate of anything greater than 7.75%), but there is always the risk that the buyer will be unable or unwilling to make the subsequent payments over time. This is of course an exaggerated example, but it makes the point: transaction structure is a critical component to overall deal value.

Asset Purchase v. Stock Purchase. One question with significant tax and legal implications that is often neglected until later in purchase negotiations is this: is the buyer purchasing the stock (equity) of the seller, or only purchasing specified assets of the seller? From a tax and liability perspective, depending on the corporate structure of the seller, the answer to this question can change the value of the deal dramatically.

For example, in the case of a C-corporation, an asset sale in most cases will be taxed twice: first at the corporate level on the asset sale itself based on the difference between the purchase price and the book value of the purchased assets. Second, the distribution from the corporation to its shareholders of the proceeds will be treated as a taxable dividend. In the case of partnerships, S-corporations, or limited liability corporations (LLC's), an asset sale is only taxed once on the gain from the sale of assets, but be aware that some state and local governments impose a transfer tax on assets of specific types (equipment or vehicles, for example).

Independent of whether your business is a C-corporation or not, the tax consequences that result from various deal structures can be significant, so make sure you speak with your tax counsel well ahead of committing to any specific transaction structure.

One other significant issue resulting from an asset versus a stock purchase is how certain liabilities are treated. Liabilities can take the form of bank loans (which can be characterized as either long-term liabilities if they mature in more than one year, and short-term liabilities in the case of many working capital lines of credit), accounts payable, accrued expenses, and contingent or unknown liabilities such as environmental, legal, or other liabilities. In a stock purchase, the buyer typically takes all assets and all liabilities of the company, whether known or unknown, which of course increases the potential risk of the transaction to the buyer.

Conversely, in an asset purchase, the buyer can list the specific assets and liabilities it is willing to take, with any remaining assets or liabilities (particularly contingent liabilities) remaining with the selling company. As a result, the seller may continue to have liability for issues that arise after closing, like an environmental or warranty claim. As a seller, you need to be aware of existing and potential liabilities and how a purchase will or will not relieve you or your business of those liabilities.

Contingent Payments and Earn-outs. In addition to the overall purchase structure, the manner in which a seller receives consideration is also critically important. For example, in most deals, it is somewhat unusual to see all of the consideration (a legal term for what you receive in exchange for your company) in the form of cash at closing. Typically, sophisticated buyers will hold something back, either in the form of a note or debt instrument, an escrow account used to satisfy breaches of representations and warranties, or in the form of an "earn-out." An "earn-out" is a payment promised by the buyer to be paid in the future based on the future performance of the business.

In many cases, an earn-out will be tied to the future cash flow of the business in some way, with some of it being taken away if the company's performance falls below certain hurdles or benchmarks, and potentially increasing if the company exceeds expectations by some margin. An earn-out means you will not receive 100% of the consideration for the deal up front, so even if your company is valued at $5 million, you might only see $3 million in cash at closing, with the remaining $2 million paid out over time (and it will be at risk of non-payment based on the company's performance).

In addition, while a seller's note might enjoy some level of priority as described above in our discussion on capital structures, it is possible that an earn-out obligation may not enjoy any priority other than as a general creditor, placing it behind other debt obligations and subjecting the earn-out to an increased risk of non-payment.

It is critical to discuss these potential deal structures with your advisors to ensure that you account for this in your cash flow projections. Once you have vetted the different deal structure possibilities with your transaction advisors, you should review these with your personal financial advisor so that you can make a decision as to whether it even makes sense to take your company to market. Too often we see sellers make a decision to go to market (which is expensive both in terms of time and money) only to later realize they have underestimated their financial requirements following closing and that there is no realistic possibility of their financial needs being met by a probable transaction. This is easily prevented with proper planning.

Employment and Consulting Agreements. Other non-financial terms you must be prepared to evaluate are the terms of employment or consulting contracts. With respect to employment or consulting contracts, buyers like to use these to tie sellers to the business for a specific period of time to help ensure the transition of operations from seller to buyer goes as smoothly as possible. Sometimes the success of the transition can be tied to an earn-out as described above, or it might be tied to the terms of an employment or consulting contract.

In situations where the seller is individually responsible for a material portion of the selling company's sales or revenues, a buyer might require the seller to enter into an employment contract or consulting contract, the responsibilities of which are to continue selling efforts and transition key relationships to the new buyer. As above, when you are considering your cash requirements and sources following a closing, be sure to consider the terms of any employment or consulting contract as these can provide a source of income for a limited period of time.

With our selling clients, we often use these components as a way to offset risk and to funnel more value to the business owner. Depending on the nature of the transaction and the buyer's and seller's desires, these can range from three months to five years or more. In addition, as with any other contract, you will want to pay particular attention to bonus structure and metrics, reporting structure, daily duties, and other terms as these will impact you for the duration of the employment contract. The discussion with a potential buyer about your future employment relationship is a healthy dialogue to have and from which you can learn a lot. We recommend sellers have this discussion as soon as is practicable.

Non-Compete Agreements. As you contemplate your future sources of income after a sale of your company, you might be considering re-entering the same business or industry after some period of time. Many sellers think this is a natural path because of their extensive industry experience. However, we generally advise clients, at least when contemplating a sale, to commit themselves to exiting the industry altogether so there is no hint created in a buyer's mind that they might see the seller in the market again anytime soon. This impression in a buyer's mind will only impair the likelihood of a deal closing or lower the valuation a buyer is willing to pay.

Sophisticated buyers will typically require a seller to execute a "non-compete agreement," which is an agreement by the seller that he will not compete in the same or similar industry within a specific geographic region for a specified period of time. In general, we see non-compete agreements lasting anywhere from one to five years with standard agreements in the two- to three-year range. Typically they will apply to the geographic area and industry sector in which a company is operating at closing. Non-compete agreements will typically appear in two places: (1) the purchase agreement for the company, because non-competes are generally more enforceable in a court of law when they are made in connection with the sale of a business, and (2) employment or consulting contracts, although these non-compete agreements are typically more limited in scope and duration.

As you plan your future post-closing, unless it is something you have discussed with the buyer (for example, you might be in the manufacturing business and want to start up a distributorship for the same product, which some buyers might not have a problem with), don't count on earning any income from a business that is related to the one you are selling, at least for some time.

CHAPTER 14

THE COMMUNICATION PLAN –
DON'T MAKE THIS MISTAKE

A sale transaction is a major event for a company, and as such, many different people have an interest in what happens – this includes your employees, suppliers, customers, business partners, shareholders, lenders, and others. Working with your advisors, make a list of all the potential constituents who would be impacted by a sale or who would want to know the details of the sale, and what your communication plan will be, before, during, and after a transaction. You should anticipate that sometime during the process, one or more of these constituents will ask you about the sale process, even though you have made every effort to keep the transaction confidential. Have a plan in place ahead of time on how to address these questions so that when it happens you are not caught completely off guard. We find that doing some role-playing with our clients helps them prepare for these conversations.

Communication with Managers. As we discussed previously, on occasion our clients will ask whether they should generally disclose the fact that a transaction is going to occur prior to closing. Again, our advice is to wait until closing to ensure the transaction actually closes before announcing the deal to employees, customers, or suppliers. However, in many transactions a buyer will want to talk with key employees during due diligence to get comfortable with the next layer of management.

In addition, buyers will want access to company financial officers to help them understand the financials in more detail and to run different reports. With these employees, it is likely that you will have to disclose to them what is happening early in the process. Assuming you have a good relationship with them, and even if you do not, this conversation can be handled well with appropriate care.

For example, we had a seller who wanted to sell his company and did not want to work for the buyer for any protracted period following closing. As a result, it was very important for the buyer to meet and get comfortable with the owner's general manager, whom our client had not yet informed he was selling the business. We recommended a set of talking points to our client that included highlighting the new opportunities available for the employee and the company with a new buyer.

As is often the case with sellers, our client had reached a point in his life where he was no longer interested in investing the level of time and money into his business as he once was, which was limiting the growth potential of the company and its employees. The opportunities with the new buyer included both personal career development as well as potential growth for the business itself with new ownership. In addition to highlighting the positives of a deal, we also made sure to have our clients caution their key employee that a deal may or may not happen (it is the deal business, after all). This is important to help manage expectations with the employee so that if a transaction does not happen, the employee is prepared for it.

As a business owner, remember that the discussion with your key management team members is not about you or your retirement objectives or how a sale will help you accomplish your individual goals. The conversation with managers should be all about them as individuals: how the transaction will help them financially, with their careers, and with their personal goals. No matter how important you think you are as a leader to them, in almost all cases, it comes down to how the transaction could affect them personally.

Even if a buyer does not intend to retain a key employee for a long period, buyers will often agree to a "stay bonus" or a bonus paid to the employee for staying with the business for a predetermined period of time following closing to help with the transition of ownership to the new owner. This can help alleviate a key employee's concerns and give the key employee time to plan for his or her future, including updating their resume and networking. Giving a key employee time to plan for their next career is always a better approach than surprising them.

Communication with Employees. Your communication plan with key managers is different, however, from your communication plan with employees in general. The general employee population of most businesses is not sophisticated with respect to transactions and acquisitions, and it is unlikely they will be able to understand and appreciate the nuances of why deals succeed or fail. We have witnessed too many occasions where an owner felt compelled to talk with the employee population at large, only to experience significant headaches from repeated questions, concerns, anxiety, and the resulting lack of focus on the operations of the business. As a result, our advice with respect to the general employee population is not to disclose any information to them until the deal closes. You should, however, work with your advisors to develop a strategy for how you will answer an employee's question when it comes up.

Communication with Customers, Suppliers and Other Key Stakeholders. Similarly, with key customers and other stakeholders, the buyer may want to speak with them ahead of time as part of their due diligence. While understandable, we always require that these discussions happen at the end of the due diligence period and after contracts have been negotiated so that there is less risk of the transaction not occurring. In addition, we like to work with buyers to craft a plausible story, such as the buyer is a new financing source for the company, which will hopefully not cause the customer or stakeholder major concerns. The goal is to balance the due diligence needs of the buyer with your needs to maintain relative equilibrium with your employers, customers, suppliers, and other stakeholders. This is possible only with careful planning and disciplined management of the process.

Communication Planning with the Buyer. As a seller, you will want to work carefully with the buyer and both sides' attorneys on the overall transaction communication plan. In order to have an effective plan, you and the buyer need to be on the same page as it relates to key messages, and you both want to make sure your communications do not subject you to undue legal risk. If your message is different from the buyer's message, your audience will pick up on this fact quickly and your communication plan will be less effective. You will also want to agree in advance with the buyer on answers to expected "frequently asked questions," which we suggest be reduced to writing to eliminate any misinterpretation. You should also agree on the overall goals of the communication plan. Typically these range from retaining employees and customers to highlighting the new strategy for all constituents.

If you are aligned with the buyer on the goals of the communication plan, the key messages you want your audience to take away, and answers to expected questions, your message will be much more effective. We advise clients to spend time thinking through this plan and then schedule the different communication sessions (first to employees, then to customers, and then to suppliers, and only then to the press, for example) so that the message does not get out ahead of you.

On some occasions, other than communicating the deal to key employees, very little communication will be required because the post-closing business will continue to run exactly as it had been run before. This type of "no change" communication can be effective, for example, when the exiting owners have key relationships that need to be transitioned carefully over time (versus a "flash cut" transition to new owners where these relationships could be at risk). In general, though, think through your communication plan ahead of time, plan carefully, and make sure you are aligned with the buyer. Only then should you execute any form of communications.

In our experience, the communication plan is one of the most important aspects of minimizing distraction to sellers, yet it is often given less attention than other aspects of the deal process. When Chris managed a large communications company that was being acquired, he learned that an effective communications plan can put employees and customers at ease, but only if the messages were clear, well considered, and delivered at the appropriate time. It was critical not to be caught by surprise, which required some extensive brainstorming of all the potential questions that might come up.

CHAPTER 15

DEAL FATIGUE

I n almost every transaction, one or both parties will experience what we call "deal fatigue." We devote a chapter to this topic because of the fact that it happens in nearly every deal, and if you don't expect it and manage it, it can potentially derail what would otherwise be a solid transaction for you.

Deal fatigue is simply the exhaustion and frustration you experience going through a transaction while still trying to manage your business effectively. A successful transaction takes time, and it involves give and take from both parties. It is rare that a transaction is closed on exactly the same terms as described in a Letter of Intent, which means at some point after the Letter of Intent is executed you will have to "renegotiate" various parts of the original deal to reflect changes in the market, changes in either party's assumptions as a result of due diligence, a lack of clarity on particular terms in the Letter of Intent, or other factors. These negotiations are sometimes difficult because they involve changes in expectations – either your expectations or the other party's expectations – and this can damage your relationship or trust in the other party if not expertly handled, which in turn contributes to further challenges.

Our experience is that parties' expectations are generally highest right after a Letter of Intent is executed, and lowest about two or three weeks prior to a deal closing. We like to say that a successful deal will "die" two to three times prior to closing as either party gets frustrated enough to cease negotiating. We have had several clients execute a Letter of Intent based on certain financial assumptions in their own business which later proved to be incorrect (and typically not in a favorable direction for our client), which meant the buyer adjusted its offer price, which in turn created frustration and anxiety on the part of our client, all because the initial expectations set forth in the Letter of Intent were not met. As a result, we try to counsel clients at the time of the Letter of Intent not to get too tied to the terms in the Letter of Intent because they will often change prior to closing.

There are several things you can do to prevent deal fatigue. First and foremost, make sure your expectations are realistic. This requires you to take a hard look at your own business and its financials. Also, make sure that the buyer's assumptions going into the Letter of Intent are based on accurate financial data. Changes in your financials will create frustration and mistrust in any buyer, and as a result will likely change a buyer's offer or willingness to enter into the transaction as originally planned.

Second, make sure your advisor or investment banker does due diligence on a particular buyer to make sure the buyer is well-financed and that it has a reputation for getting transactions closed. We sometimes run into inexperienced buyers who don't have financing lined up prior to signing a Letter of Intent, which more times than not creates challenges for them during a transaction. This will often be reflected either in delays or odd negotiating tactics while they try to get their financing completed. Experienced buyers who have relationships with financing sources will have an easier time getting financed because of their prior relationships, but even in these situations, financing can be a risk to closing the deal. In addition, there are unscrupulous buyers in the market who sign a Letter of Intent, only to renegotiate its terms as they get potential sellers wedded to the transaction.

Third, prepare yourself for a tough negotiation – don't react too negatively or positively to any development during a transaction, take time to think through your position before responding to the other party, and use your advisors to help you think through various issues. In addition, try not to take the negotiation personally. This is a business transaction and you should expect the other side to try to maximize its value in the transaction, which will sometimes involve contentious negotiations.

Fourth, use your advisors to help you evaluate a transaction as objectively as possible. We often will prepare an analysis of a buyer's offer for our clients at several stages during the negotiation to help our clients understand how the buyer's offer compares to the market. For example, we once had a client whose financial condition deteriorated significantly during due diligence, which of course meant the buyer's offer changed. Our client was extremely frustrated and ready to walk away from the deal until we gave him an analysis which showed that even the revised, lower offer was a 100% premium to the value of comparable publicly-traded companies. So, by remaining objective and not "anchoring" yourself in the original offer one way or the other, you will be better able to rationally and logically understand and analyze the buyer's position during the process.

Finally, know ahead of time your "walk-away" price. This can be based on market valuations, your own personal needs, or other factors. It should not be based on the buyer's initial offer, which too often creates unrealistic expectations and therefore disappointment and frustration.

Deal fatigue will happen, and it will seem like there is no hope of getting to a resolution, but with an experienced team of advisors, you can typically work through most issues. Particularly near the final stages of a negotiation, when each party feels like it has given on all the issues it can give on, deal fatigue can substantially interfere with the closing of a deal. Be aware that it is happening, take a step back, talk with your advisors, manage your expectations, and you will be able to push through those final issues and consummate what is hopefully a solid transaction for you and your team.

CHAPTER 16

WHAT HAPPENS AT AND AFTER CLOSING?

T he actual closing of a sale transaction is somewhat anticlimactic. Typically, after the negotiations over the contracts and documentation have concluded, both the buyer and seller will sign multiple copies of the different agreements and give them to their attorneys to hold pending final agreement that the deal is closed.

Sometimes the parties will meet at one of the attorney's offices to sign the documents and officially close the transaction and work out any final details, but this is certainly not required. In most closings, the actual funds transfer happens via wire transfer from the buyer's account to the seller's account, and as the seller, you will anxiously await confirmation from your bank that the funds have hit, at which point the closing process is usually complete.

We advise our clients, even before we take them to market, to think through what they are going to do following closing. Closing the sale of your business can be an emotionally taxing time. There is often a letdown following the closing in which a business owner's daily routine changes, sometimes dramatically if there is a quick transition to the new owner and the previous owner is no longer working in the business. For these reasons, we recommend that our clients take time to map out what their first few months following closing will look like. This can include long-deferred trips, taking care of things around the house that have been ignored, spending time with family, or pursuing a personal interest or hobby. In addition, it is a good idea to have planned with your financial advisor how the proceeds from the sale will be invested so that you can implement your post-closing financial plan effectively.

The Harvest – A Reward for Years of Hard Work. You have spent years working to develop and improve your business – make sure you invest similar time and energy into the planning for the sale of your business. We are confident it will pay dividends and will make one of the most important decisions of your life easier, more fruitful, and less stressful. Above all, enjoy the closing and the time following closing – you have worked hard to build your business, so enjoy the harvest of your labor!

If you would like to discuss your company's valuation or potential exit strategies, or you would like to receive our Seller's ToolKit, which includes:

- Interactive Business Valuation Tool
- Buyer Interview Sheet
- Sample Project Timeline
- Letter of Intent Information Request
- Form of Nondisclosure Agreement
- Form of Personal Needs Interview Questionnaire

please e-mail us at:

david@capitalvalue.net
chris@capitalvalue.net

or call us at 720-733-0400.

We look forward to hearing from you.

ABOUT THE AUTHORS

David Tolson is a founder and Managing Director for Capital-Value Advisors, an investment bank in Englewood, Colorado, and the Chief Executive Officer for CapitalValue, LLC, a business valuation firm which he also founded. David has completed hundreds of business valuations in almost every industry segment, and is an accredited valuation expert, being awarded the AIBA (Accredited by the Institute of Business Appraisers) designation. Previously, David worked in Colorado's high-tech community as the lead business development officer for NeoCore, iWitness, and IQ3G, and created and led J.D. Edwards' first successful strategic business unit. David is a graduate of Colorado State University and earned an MBA (emphasis in finance) from the University of Colorado, where he was awarded the Beta Gamma Sigma designation for outstanding scholastic achievement.

Chris Younger is also a founder and Managing Director for CapitalValue Advisors, and is the Chairman and Chief Executive Officer for The Silvercloud Companies, a private equity firm in Englewood, Colorado, with investments in telecommunications, construction, and software distribution. Previously, Chris was the President and Chief Operating Officer for Expanets, which at the time was the nation's largest value added distributor of voice and data networking solutions with over $1 billion in sales. Chris helped found Expanets and was responsible for its acquisition strategy, which involved acquiring 27 companies over the course of two years. Chris is a self-described "recovering" attorney, having clerked for the Honorable Jesse E. Eschbach of the United States Court of Appeals, Seventh Circuit, and having practiced corporate law in California for Wilson, Sonsini, Goodrich, and Rosati. Chris graduated from Harvard Law School, where he was the Managing Editor of the *Harvard Law Review*, and from Miami University in Oxford, Ohio, and attended the London School of Economics where he studied jurisprudence.

GLOSSARY

Add-Backs or Adjustments	"Add-Backs," or Adjustments to Earnings, are additions to reported net income figures typically proposed by sellers for one-time expenses (e.g., unusual litigation, moving, etc.) or expenses that a buyer should not expect to incur after closing (e.g., in some cases, owner compensation if the owner will not be employed going forward, or other similar expenses). Buyers and sellers often disagree about what are truly one-time expenses (one of our favorite sayings is: "Life is a series of one-time events"), or what expenses a buyer should not expect to incur going forward (e.g., a buyer will still need to pay a manager even if the owner is departing). Whether you are a buyer or seller, be deliberate and careful in your evaluation of these types of adjustments.
Adjusted Net Book Value	Adjusted Net Book Value is the Book Value of a business that has been adjusted to reflect the current market value of the assets and liabilities of a company. For example, some companies accelerate depreciation on fixed assets for tax purposes, and the fair market value of those fixed assets might be considerably higher than what is reflected in the company's accounting records. In this case, an adjustment to the value of these assets is

required to determine Adjusted Net Book Value.

Asset Purchase Agreement

An Asset Purchase Agreement is a contract between a buyer and a seller pursuant to which the buyer purchases certain assets of the seller and assumes certain liabilities. These agreements will typically contain representations and warranties from a seller about the assets and business of the company, and will include other material transaction terms.

Asset Value

Asset Value can refer to one of two things: the book value of a specific asset (i.e., what is the value of an asset as listed on the company's accounting records), or the fair market value of a specific asset or group of assets. You may hear Asset Value used in place of Book Value, but this is not precisely correct because Book Value includes not only Asset Value, but also subtracts the value of liabilities of a company.

Balance Sheet

A Balance Sheet is an accounting record for a company that lists a company's assets, liabilities, and shareholders' equity.

Book

The "Book" in mergers and acquisitions refers to a detailed presentation about a business for sale, including information on its financials, sales, operations, employees, management, and other important information. This "Book" is typically presented to potential buyers to solicit interest in a business for sale.

Book Value | "Book Value" can refer to two different concepts: first, Book Value can refer to the value ascribed to a particular asset or liability on a company's balance sheet. Book Value can also refer to the value of a company's assets minus its liabilities as portrayed on the company's balance sheet. Book Value is often contrasted with Market Value, which reflects the value of a company's equity (assets minus liabilities) as determined by what a willing buyer would pay to a willing seller in an arm's length transaction (versus the value of a company's equity as reflected in its accounting records and balance sheet).

Buy-Sell Agreement | A Buy-Sell Agreement is an agreement between and among shareholders in a company that details the terms under which the shareholders can sell their stakes in the business (either to a third party or to one another). In particular, a Buy-Sell Agreement will typically provide for what happens in the event that one of the shareholders leaves the business and he or she needs to dispose of an equity stake in the business. A Buy-Sell Agreement can also address what happens in the event of the death or incapacity of a key shareholder, and can require that the company procure Key Man Life Insurance to fund the Buy-Sell Obligations in such event.

Capital Expense | Capital Expense or Investment is an expenditure by a company for an asset that is typically capitalized on a company's balance sheet as an asset that will be depreciated over time (versus running through a company's profit and loss statement as a current expense). Examples of Capital Expense or Investment are furniture and fixtures, real estate, computers, equipment, vehicles, and other long-lived assets.

Cash Flow Statement   The Cash Flow Statement is a financial statement that shows the true cash flow of a company (i.e., it explains the change in cash balance of a company over a period of time, as compared to simply determining net income, which may not be the same as the cash generated by the company). Utilizing the Income Statement and Balance Sheet of a company, the Cash Flow Statement explains the change in a company's cash position over time by adjusting net income for non-cash expenses such as depreciation and amortization, as well as for increases or decreases in working capital, financing (raising or repaying debt or equity investment), and fixed asset sales or purchases.

Cash-on-Cash Return   Cash-on-Cash Return is a term (sometimes also referred to as Return on Investment) used to describe the rate of return on a particular investment by comparing the actual cash generated by a company and distributed to an investor with the cash investment made by the investor. For example, if an investor received $100 in cash in a particular year after an investment of $1,000, his Cash-on-Cash Return would be 10 percent.

Common Equity	Common Equity (sometimes also referred to as Common Stock) reflects the value of a company's assets minus its liabilities minus any Preferred Equity that would have preference over the Common Equity. It is typically the highest risk/highest potential return portion of a company's capital structure.
Consulting Agreement	Consulting Agreement in the context of mergers and acquisitions refers to an agreement between a company and typically an exiting owner/seller in which the exiting owner/seller continues to provide specified consulting services to the buyer for a specified period of time. These services might be related to the core operations of the acquired business, or they may be related to the transition of ownership (e.g., transitioning key employee, customer, and supplier relationships).
Current Assets	Current Assets refers to assets such as cash, accounts receivable, inventory, and marketable securities (cash equivalents on short notice) that are used and replenished during the normal operating cycle of the business. Current Assets can be contrasted with Fixed Assets, which have a longer life and are depreciated over time.
Current Liabilities	Current Liabilities consist of items such as accounts payable, accrued liabilities, and liabilities with maturities (when the liability must be paid) of less than one year. Current Liabilities can be contrasted with Long-Term Liabilities, which have maturities of greater than one year and typi-

cally consist of debt instruments and other longer-term deferred liabilities (pension liabilities sometimes fall into this category).

Discount Rate

Discount Rate refers to the rate at which a stream of future cash flows is discounted to determine Net Present Value. The higher the degree of risk or unpredictability of a set of future cash flows, the higher the discount rate. It can also refer to the rate of return required by investors for a particular investment.

Discounted Cash Flow Value

Discounted Cash Flow Value refers to the calculation of a company's Enterprise Value on the basis of its ability to generate free cash flow over time. To compute the enterprise value, the free cash flows are discounted back to present value at a rate that reflects the risk as estimated by the buyer or seller (which rates will often differ based on their respective assessments of the level of risk in a company).

Due Diligence

Due Diligence refers to the process by which a buyer evaluates a seller's company. Due Diligence will involve a review of the company's financials and key documents and contracts, interviews with management and other key employees, customer and supplier reference checks, market research, and other processes designed to help the buyer understand and evaluate the seller's business.

EBITDA

EBITDA refers to Earnings Before deducting Interest, Taxes, Depreciation, and

Amortization costs, and is often used by buyers and sellers as a proxy for operating cash flow in a business (i.e., the cash flow generated by the business prior to paying interest expenses, taxes, or incurring capital expenditures).

EBITDA Multiple

EBITDA Multiple refers to the multiple of EBITDA used to determine a company's enterprise value. This is often used by buyers and sellers as a short-cut to determining the value of a company (prior to deducting any long-term debt a company owes). Buyers and sellers should be careful when using these "rules of thumb," as they often mask underlying risks and opportunities in a business which can increase or decrease the value of a company.

Employment Agreement

Employment Agreement, similar to a Consulting Agreement, in the context of mergers and acquisitions refers to an agreement with either the seller or one of the seller's key employees regarding the terms and conditions of his or her employment with the new buyer. These terms and conditions can include salary, bonus programs, benefits, payments in the event of a termination of employment, non-compete and confidentiality provisions, as well as other terms and conditions.

Enterprise Value

Enterprise Value refers to the overall value of a company (including both equity and debt). Valuations of a company are often done as an Enterprise Value, from which you would need to subtract any Long-Term Debt or other longer-term liabilities to determine the Equity Value of a company.

Equity Value
: Equity Value refers to the value of the equity in a company, and is typically determined by subtracting the amount of Long-Term Debt or other longer-term liabilities from the Enterprise Value of a company. Equity Value typically refers only to the value of the Common Equity in a company, but can also include Preferred Equity.

Exclusivity Clause
: An Exclusivity Clause is a provision in a Letter of Intent or Indication of Interest in which a seller agrees that it will not solicit interest in its business from or talk to third party potential bidders other than the buyer for a specified period of time. This provision is generally granted by sellers to buyers in exchange for the buyer's commitment to expend time and resources conducting Due Diligence prior to signing a formal Asset or Stock Purchase Agreement. Exclusivity Clauses can run anywhere from a few days at the minimum to two months or more, and they are often extended during the Due Diligence process if it takes longer than anticipated.

Financial Buyer
: Financial Buyer refers to buyers who buy primarily based on financial returns and may be indifferent with respect to the industries in which they invest. Financial Buyer also refers to investors such as private equity firms, buyout firms, venture

capital firms, or other professionally managed funds of capital. Financial Buyers are typically contrasted with Strategic Buyers who are not professional money managers, but who are industry players interested in using mergers and acquisitions to help them grow, expand geographically, or otherwise complement their core business strategies.

Free Cash Flow

Free Cash Flow refers to the amount of cash generated by a business after all of its operating expenses, capital investments, and disposals have been accounted for, and after accounting for changes in working capital (whether positive or negative). It can be calculated on a pre- or post-tax basis.

Hybrid Buyer

Hybrid Buyer refers to a buyer who is a cross between a Financial Buyer and a Strategic Buyer. Often these are companies that are being financed by a private equity or investment firm to do a "roll-up," or series of acquisitions in a particular industry.

Income Statement

Income Statement refers to the financial statement of operations of a company in which revenues, cost of sales, and operating expenses are presented to calculate the Net Income of a company.

Indication of Interest

Indication of Interest is typically a letter (sometimes an e-mail) from a potential buyer expressing its interest in acquiring a particular seller. Typically non-binding on either party and similar to a Letter of

Intent, an Indication of Interest will spell out a buyer's proposed valuation range, transaction structure, and other material terms of a potential transaction. These are used early in the acquisition process to help buyer and seller come to an agreement on the particular terms of a transaction, and may include Exclusivity Clauses which forbid the seller from contacting other potential buyers for a period of time.

Lehman Formula

Lehman Formula refers to the formula (originally established by Lehman Brothers) that determines the commission to be earned by an investment bank, mergers and acquisitions advisor, business broker, or other transaction intermediary as a result of procuring a buyer for a seller's business. These clauses are typically found in representation agreements between the seller and an intermediary charged with taking the seller's business to market.

Letter of Intent

Letter of Intent – see Indication of Interest. The Letter of Intent is sometimes more detailed than the Indication of Interest, but the general purpose is the same.

Long-Term Liabilities

Long-Term Liabilities refer to liabilities on a company's balance sheet with maturities or due dates of longer than one year.

Market Value

Market Value refers to the value placed on an asset (or company) in the open market by a willing buyer from a willing seller in an arm's-length transaction. Market Value is typically distinguished from Book Value, which is the value as reflected on the company's financial statement or accounting records and may not reflect actual fair market value.

Multiple of Earnings

Multiple of Earnings, similar to Multiple of EBITDA, refers to the multiple of a company's earnings to establish the entity valuation of the company. This can be compared to a Price to Earnings Ratio, although the Price to Earnings Ratio typically refers to the Equity Value of a company divided by its net, after-tax income.

Multiple of Revenues

Multiple of Revenues, similar to Multiple of Earnings and Multiple of EBITDA, refers to a valuation based on a multiple of a company's revenues to establish overall Enterprise valuation. This type of valuation is sometimes used for companies that are early in their life cycle and do not yet have operating earnings (as was sometimes the case for early Internet companies), or when looking at overall market valuations where the Multiple of Earnings or Multiple of EBITDA valuation ranges are too wide to rely on.

Net Income

Net Income can refer either to pre- or post-tax net earnings of a company, which is defined as revenues or sales, less cost of sales, less operating expenses, less interest, and either before or after taxes.

Normalized Earnings

Normalized Earnings (see Add-Back) refers to the Net Income of a company that has been adjusted by adding back non-recurring expenses or expenses a buyer should not expect to incur after an acquisition. In this sense, the earnings are adjusted to reflect these one-time or non-recurring expenses.

One-Time Expenses

One-Time Expenses refer to expenses that are expected to occur only once. For example, a company that has incurred moving expenses from relocating offices might legitimately claim these are one-time expenses that will not be incurred on an ongoing basis (unless, of course, moving is a part of their business). Similarly, a company that was involved in major litigation only once in its existence (depending on the reason for the litigation, of course), might claim these are One-Time Expenses. Buyers and sellers will debate these items intensely as they have an impact on overall valuation for a company.

Option

An Option (see Warrant, and sometimes referred to as a "Call Option") is the right of the holder of the Option to purchase shares of equity in a business at a fixed price for a set period of time. Options are valuable to the extent the exercise price is lower than the fair market value of the underlying shares, or where the option period is long enough that there is plenty of time for the underlying share value to grow past the exercise price of the Option.

Owner Compensation

Owner Compensation refers to the overall compensation an owner receives from a business. This can include not only salary and bonus, but also benefits such as cars, insurance payments, benefits, or other "perks" the owner has received that have been paid for by the company. Often sellers will argue for Owner Compensation to qualify as an Add-Back, but careful buyers will understand that some of these expenses may in fact be required to attract a new manager going forward.

Preferred Equity

Preferred Equity represents equity in a company that has a liquidation preference over Common Equity and will often have a dividend payment. It is the second-most risky portion of a company's capital structure (after Common Equity), but can enjoy appreciation potential similar to Common Equity depending on the terms and conditions of the Preferred Equity.

Price/Earnings Multiple

Price/Earnings Multiple is a valuation methodology typically used in valuing publicly held companies. It refers to the ratio calculated by dividing a company's equity value (or share price) by its after-tax earnings (or earnings per share). The higher the P/E Ratio, the higher the valuation of a company's equity.

Recurring Revenues (versus One-Time Revenues)

Recurring Revenues (versus One-Time Revenues) refers to revenues of a company that can be expected to be generated on a regular basis over time (versus One-Time Revenues that are typically only expected to happen once). An example of Recurring Revenues would be the revenues a telecommunications company earns from its customers that have three year contracts to purchase their telecommunications requirements – these revenues are expected to recur (at least over the three-year period). An example of One-Time Revenues would be the revenues a construction company receives from a specific project which has a defined beginning and end. Buyers will typically place higher value on Recurring Revenue businesses than on businesses where the revenues are One-Time or project based because Recurring Revenues are more predictable.

Return on Investment | Return on Investment (see Cash-on-Cash Return) refers to the rate of return an investor generates on an investment.

Secured Debt | Secured Debt refers to debt of a company that is secured by the company's assets (such as accounts receivable, inventory, and fixed assets). In the event of a liquidation or bankruptcy of the company, Secured Debt holders have first claim to those assets and the proceeds from their sale, and hence enjoy a relatively senior position in the company's capital structure, but typically have lower expected rates of return than for Common Equity or Preferred Equity.

Senior Secured Debt | Senior Secured Debt is Secured Debt but has a senior claim to all other debt holders on the assets of the company. Senior Secured Debt occupies the safest portion of a company's capital structure.

Short-Term Liabilities | Short-Term Liabilities refer generally to accounts payable, current portions of long-term debt, and other liabilities that are due or mature in less than one year.

Stock Purchase Agreement

Stock Purchase Agreement (see Asset Purchase Agreement) is an agreement that sets forth the terms under which a buyer purchases stock or shares in a company from a seller. It will have similar terms and conditions to an Asset Purchase Agreement, with the major difference being the buyer in a Stock Purchase Agreement generally assumes all liabilities (whether known or unknown) in the company, whereas an asset purchase allows a buyer to exclude certain known and unknown liabilities from what he is assuming.

Strategic Buyer

Strategic Buyer is a buyer typically in the same, related, or "surrounding" industry as a seller and who is interested in purchasing companies in its own industry or related industries for a strategic reason (i.e., consolidation, geographic expansion, product line extension, or other reasons such as these).

Subordinated Debt

Subordinated Debt is debt of a company that is subordinate to Senior Debt. Subordinated Debt in the event of a liquidation is paid before any equity (whether Common Equity or Preferred Equity), but is paid after Senior Debt.

Warrant

Warrant (see Option) is the right of the holder of the Warrant to purchase shares of equity in a business at a fixed price for a set period of time. Warrants are valuable to the extent the exercise price is lower than the fair market value of the underlying shares, or where the option period is long enough that there is plenty of time for the underlying share value to grow past the exercise price of the Warrant.

Working Capital

Working Capital is defined as Current Assets minus Current Liabilities and represents the investment in a company required to operate the business during its cash cycle (the time between when a company incurs and pays its expenses and the time it receives payment for its products or services).

APPENDIX A

FORM OF REQUEST FOR PROPOSAL

This Example of a Request for Proposal is something we encourage you to use when evaluating potential transaction advisors to help you in your selling process.

Form of Request for Proposal

1. Confidentiality is paramount. Describe how you would safeguard confidentiality throughout the entire process, including the RFQ process.

2. Provide General Information about your firm and services it provides – include any brochures, website addresses, or other information you deem appropriate.

3. Explain what differentiates you from other firms who may have more industry expertise.

4. Describe your firm's general philosophy, values, and approach to representation services.

5. Describe the process by which you intend to market our business.

6. Describe the process by which you will identify and target potential strategic buyers for our business.

7. Describe the overall process by which you intend to manage the acquisition, including a proposed timeline from engagement to projected close date that details each significant step in the acquisition process.

8. Please provide names, resumes, and backgrounds and specific experience and specific roles of the personnel from your firm who will represent us. In addition, describe the typical level of involvement at each stage of the acquisition process for each person participating in your firm. In particular, describe each person's experience in negotiations, valuation, completing transactions, and other experience you believe is relevant. It is important that we understand exactly who we will be working with.

APPENDIX B

DUE DILIGENCE INFORMATION REQUEST LIST

The following Due Diligence Information Request List is typical of due diligence lists buyers give to sellers to gather information about the seller to help the buyer evaluate the seller's business.

Due Diligence Request List

Please provide copies of all items listed or indicate "N/A" for those that are <u>not</u> applicable. Please compile and deliver copies of all documents which are requested or which respond to the items below. It is very important that entire documents (front and back) be copied. Please call if you do not understand the request or have any concerns you would like to share.

1. CORPORATE/OPERATIONAL MATTERS

(A)   Articles of Incorporation together with all amendments

(B)   Bylaws as amended and currently in effect

(C)   Stock Certificates and Stock Book (including copies of the front and back of all stock certificates including cancelled certificates), stock transfer records, and all documents relating to stock ownership including a list of all outstanding options, warrants, or other rights relating to the stock

(D)   Minutes of Board of Directors Meetings and any committees thereof (or written consents in lieu thereof)

(E)   Minutes of Shareholder's Meetings (or written consents in lieu thereof)

(F)   Shareholder's Agreements, including Buy-Sell or Stock Redemption Agreements; stock options or conversion rights

(G)   Voting Agreements, proxies, powers of attorney

(H)   All agreements, arrangements, or understandings by Company or its shareholders to issue, purchase, or sell any securities of the Company

(I)   List of Shareholders, including number of shares and percent of ownership

(J)   List of current Board of Directors

(K)   List of current Officers

(L)   All licenses, permits, and certificates from regulatory authorities

(M)   List of all jurisdictions outside home state where Company has facilities or authority to transact business. Has company "qualified" to do business in each state?

(N)   List of all locations where the Company maintains offices (owned or leased), facilities, or employees, pays any kind of taxes on a recurring basis to solicit or perform business, identifying the nature and function of each location including the street address of each

(O)   Good Standing certificates for the state of incorporation and business qualification certificates for each foreign jurisdiction in which the Company is qualified

(P)   List of any subsidiaries or related companies in which officers, directors, or shareholders or their families have an interest, including name, state of incorporation, and capitalization

(Q)   List of all partnerships, joint ventures, or affiliates

(R)   List of professional advisors and consultants including attorneys, accountants, marketing and advertising firms

(S)   List of ten largest customers and suppliers and related contracts

(T)   All business plans prepared by or for the Company in the last two years

(U)   All projections, forecasts, and budgets (including capital budgets) prepared by or for the Company in the last two years, including all assumptions integral thereto

(V)   All studies, reports, analyses, summaries, or memoranda prepared by or for the Company in the last two years (for any purpose) relating to the Company's business operations, prospects, or financing

(W)   Independent valuation or appraisals of the Company's capital stock and/or its assets

(X)   List of any related party activities, i.e., related party contracts, Agreements, and leases

2. EMPLOYEE MATTERS

(A)   List of all employees by:
- Position/title
- Compensation/annual
- Commission/commission plan
- Full- or part-time status
- Date of hire
- Accrued vacation, sick time, etc.
- Other eligible benefits, i.e., automobile, cell phone, pager, cafeteria plan

(B)   Organization chart with reporting responsibilities

(C)   Employment, consulting, commission, and independent con-

155

tractor agreements

(D)   Confidentiality, non-compete, and trade secret agreements with present and former employees

(E)   Employee handbooks and employment and personnel policies and procedures (both written and informal policies), including separation pay (severance)

(F)   Union or collective bargaining agreements

(G)   Unfair labor practice or labor law violations

(H)   Subcontractor Labor Agreements or Outsourcing Service Agreements

(I) Pension, profit-sharing 401(k) Plan:
- Plan Document
- Summary Plan Description
- Summary of Material Modifications
- Related Trust Agreements
- Group Annuity Contract
- IRS Form 5500 and Schedules for the last three (3) years
- Most recent actuarial report
- IRS Determination Letter
- ADP/ACP Testing Reports for the last three (3) years

(J)   Deferred compensation plans and salary continuation plans

(K)   Stock option plans, including a list of each employee who has been granted options and the number of shares subject to the option

(L)   Bonus plans or arrangements

(M)   Incentive compensation plans and phantom stock plans

(N)   Severance agreements, arrangements, or policies

(O)   List of all employees entitled to or receiving COBRA benefits

(P)   Other Employee Benefits:
- Medical, dental, vision
- Life, disability insurance
- Retirement benefits
- Medical reimbursement
- "Cafeteria"
- Tuition Reimbursement
- Savings Programs
- Automobiles or automobile allowances
- Club membership
- Telephone services
- Computers
- Other incentives

3. <u>CONTRACTS, AGREEMENTS, AND ARRANGEMENTS</u>

(A)   Contracts and agreements with manufacturers, distributors, customers, vendors, suppliers (i.e., preferred vendor or supplier contracts)

(B)   Sales, supply, service, maintenance, or requirements agreements (including long-term agreements)

(C)   Government contracts, Minority Entitlement Contracts

(D)   Any forms of express warranties and disclaimers of warranty made by the Company during the past five years and a summary of any breach of representation claims against the Company during the past five (5) years

(E)   Joint venture/partnership agreements

(F)   Agreements with advertising/public relations agencies

(G)   Performance or customs bonds

(H)   Powers of attorney

(I)   Research and development contracts

(J)   Agreements with investment bankers, brokers, and other in-
termediaries

(K)   Agreements restricting the conduct of the company or its business

(L)   Letters of intent

(M)   Personal property leases (i.e. equipment and computer leases,
maintenance leases, telephone leases, leases of photocopy machines,
postage meters, and automobiles)

(N)   Other contracts, agreements, and arrangements, including descriptions of all the foregoing that are <u>oral</u>

(O)   Standard company business forms (i.e., purchase orders and
invoices)

(P)   All indemnification agreements

4. PERSONAL PROPERTY

(A)   Any and all bills of sale, leases, and other agreements to purchase or lease personal property (together with financing and security
arrangements)

(B)   Schedule of all tangible personal property such as machinery,
equipment, vehicles, furniture, and fixtures, including but not limited
to the following:
- Owned or leased status
- Financing agreement or lease contracts
- Date acquired
- Summary of insurance in force

5. <u>REAL PROPERTY</u>

(A)   <u>Owned real property</u> - Provide the following information for <u>each parcel</u> of owned real property:

- Transfer Deed
- Location/Address, including the county
- Name of record owner
- Deeds of Trusts/other encumbrances (i.e., purchase option agreements)
- Encroachments or boundary disputes
- Title insurance policy
- Any "Phase I" or other environmental assessment, audit, or other study
- Zoning letters
- Building code restrictions
- Inspection reports
- Appraisals
- Surveys
- Copies of leases between the company, as lessor, and the third parties for land not used by the company

(B)   <u>Leased real property</u> - all lease documents, including:

- Location/Address, including the county
- Name, address, and phone number of lessor and/or property manager
- Lease Agreement with all amendments
- Any subleases or assignments of leases
- Deeds of Trust and other encumbrances or liens
- Was it originally owned by you, then sold and leased back?
- Purchase options or rights of first refusal

6. __INTELLECTUAL PROPERTY__

(A)   List of all patents, trademarks, service marks, or copyrights issued or applied for, including the name of the record owners and the registration/application number

(B)   List of all trade names used by the company and registered jurisdiction, if any (current and discontinued)

(C)   Patent/trademark/copyright licensing agreements (company as licensee or licensor; royalties paid out or received)

(D)   Infringement actions or challenges to ownership (pending or threatened)

(E)   Inventory of computer systems (hardware and software), including copies of all leases and licenses

(F)   Other agreements respecting trade secrets or confidential designs or information

7. __INDEBTEDNESS__

(A)   List of all banking and credit activities and relationships by bank name, account number, account type and/or purpose, authorized signer

(B)   All agreements related to indebtedness for borrowed money or trade credit:
  - Loan and Credit Agreements
  - Promissory Notes
  - Financing Statements
  - Security Agreements
  - Pledge Agreements
  - Subordination Agreements
  - Deeds of Trust

(C)   List of all guarantees or indemnity contracts in connection with obligations of the company, including personal guarantees

(D)   Letters of Credit

(E)   Revolving credit agreements/line of credit

(F)   Lease-purchase agreements
- Automobiles
- Equipment

(G)   Equity purchase agreements/arrangements

8. LITIGATION

(A)   List of all pending or threatened legal proceedings and all files related thereto; investigations, grievance proceedings, arbitration, or mediation

(B)   All settlement agreements, court orders, or judgments, threatened litigation, or asserted claims

(C)   List of all potential claims (asserted or unasserted, liquidated or contingent), i.e., discrimination, products liability

(D)   Summary of all administrative proceedings, claims, or investigations by or before federal, state, or local governmental bodies (i.e., OSHA, EPA)

9. INSURANCE

(A)   All insurance certificates and schedule of insurance policies, coverage, expiration dates, rate, and summary of claims history:
- Health
- Vehicles
- Property
- Liability
- Business interruption and discontinuance
- Key Man

- Other

(B)   List of any pending uninsured claims indicating whether and to what extent any reserves have been established in the financial statements of the Company

(C)   All outstanding workers compensation claims

(D)   Insurance claims loss runs for the last five (5) years, including:
- General commercial liability
- Workers compensation

10. GOVERNMENTAL COMPLIANCE

(A)   Describe the Company's compliance or noncompliance with applicable governmental regulations. Possible regulated areas of the Company's business include:
- Health, safety, labeling of products
- Health and safety in company's plants and facilities
- Equal Employment Opportunity
- Wages and hours of employment
- Environmental protection and pollution controls (including hazardous waste disposal)
- Pricing, sale, and distribution of products
- Import/export permits or licenses
- Interstate Commerce Commission requirements
- Unclaimed property, including customer deposits

(B)   List any governmental or non-governmental agencies (such as Underwriter's Laboratories) which regulate or affect the Company's business

(C)   Federal, state, and local permits, authorizations, registrations, licenses, or qualifications necessary for the conduct of the Company's business. List the name of the government agency, type of license, expiration date, and whether it is assignable or transferable

(D)   Any violations cited in inspections by Federal, State, or local regulatory agencies (e.g., EPA, OSHA, FDA, USDA, etc.) in the last year

11. TAX

(A)   Income tax returns for the last five (5) years:
- Federal
- State
- Local

(B)   Last three years' sales and use tax returns (grouped by jurisdiction)

(C)   Last three years' payroll and unemployment tax returns:
- Federal
- State

(D)   List of all states where the Company is registered to collect sales and use taxes

(E)   List of all out-of-state customers for whom sales and use taxes are withheld

(F)   All correspondence from IRS or Department of Revenue as to audits or disputes

12. FINANCIAL INFORMATION

(A)   Historical financial statements together with accountants' opinions (audit, review, or compilation) for last three (3) years

(B)   Monthly financial statements for each month of current fiscal year

(C)   Year-to-date financial statements for the current fiscal year

(D)   Detailed accounts receivable aging and reconciliation to general ledger

(E)   Credit issues and analysis of bad debt expense and write-offs for the last three (3) years

(F)   Detailed inventory list by department and by item (units and value) and reconciliation to general ledger

(G)   Analysis of inventory write-offs/obsolescence (including write-downs for last three years)

(H)   Detailed accounts payable aging and reconciliation to general ledger

(I)   Detail of accrued liabilities and reconciliation to general ledger

(J)   Schedule of notes and loans receivable

(K)   Schedule of notes and loans payable (with copies of all notes and agreements) for the three (3) most recent fiscal years, and the most recent period including copies of the following:

- Any and all outstanding bonds, notes, debentures, trust indentures, loan agreements, bank credit lines (whether or not drawn upon), guarantees, or other indebtedness, and all amendments, consents, and waivers related thereto, as well as a list of all lenders or holders and certificates to the lenders or the holders during the past three (3) years
- Any and all documents and agreements evidencing other material financing arrangements, such as sale and leaseback arrangements, capitalized leases, and installment purchases
- Any and all bad debts and any agreements which might reasonably be expected to result in a loss
- All warranties, guarantees, and other obligations given or incurred by the Company or any of its subsidiaries

(L)   Schedule of prepaid expenses

(M)   Schedule of all bank accounts (operating, savings, or invest-ment), certificates of deposit, and safe deposit boxes, including the following information:
- Name and address of institution
- Account number
- Purpose of account
- Authorized signer
- Current month-end balance

(N)   General ledger, sales journals, cash receipts journals for last fiscal year

(O)   A breakdown of the officers' and other salary components of general and administrative expenses for the last three fiscal years and for the most recent period

(P)   Description of accounting policies, estimates, and methods used and any changes to these

(Q)   Written documentation of the Company's accounting system/procedures/controls relating to:
- Cash receipts
- Cash disbursements
- Payroll
- Credit, billings, and collections
- Purchasing procedures
- Production (including quality control)
- Distribution
- Sales
- Budgeting process
- Financial reporting
- Management Information Systems

(R)   Detail fixed asset schedule (furniture, fixtures, equipment, automobiles) with historical cost, accumulated depreciation, including recent appraisals of assets, if any, and reconciliation to general ledger

(S)   Management letters (internal control letters from auditors; copies of attorneys' audit letters)

(T)   Recent projections including forecasted balance sheets, income and cash flow statements, and assumptions upon which the forecasts are based

(U)   List and description of any other liabilities or obligations (including contingent ones) not reflected in the interim financial statements or incurred in the ordinary course of business since the date of the last financial statements

APPENDIX C

In reviewing a set of financial statements, sophisticated buyers and analysts will calculate a series of ratios that help assess the health of a business. While by no means exhaustive, we have included below a number of different ratios, how they are calculated, and what they mean, for your reference. As a company owner, it is good to understand these ratios and what they indicate about the health of your business.

These ratios deal principally with a company's balance sheet – specifically, how solid is a company's financial footing. One of the key measures of how secure a business might be is a measurement of liquidity, which is a measure of the quality and adequacy of current assets to meet current obligations as they come due. In other words, is a company able to convert its assets to cash in order to meet its immediate and short-term obligations without sacrificing value? For firms with recurring revenues or other predictable cash flows, liquidity is not nearly as critical as it is for firms like contracting or manufacturing businesses whose revenue streams can vary dramatically over time. The following ratios give you tools to help assess a company's liquidity:

Current Ratio: A company's current ratio is an approximation of a company's ability to pay its current obligations. The higher the current ratio, generally the better equipped a company is to manage its current obligations. As with all calculations, it is critical to evaluate the strength of the current assets used to calculate the current ratio (for example, cash is very liquid and can readily be used to pay off current obligations, whereas accounts receivable or inventory may take more time to convert to cash). The calculation for a company's Current Ratio is:

$$\frac{\text{Total Current Assets}}{\text{Total Current Liabilities}}$$

Quick Ratio: Also called the "Acid Test," and similar to the Current Ratio, a company's Quick Ratio is a more conservative way to calculate a company's near-term liquidity as it includes as Current Assets only cash and trade receivables (or their equivalents), which are assets most easily converted to cash at an amount near their book value. As a result, this ratio will typically be lower than the Current Ratio calculated above. As a rule of thumb, if the Quick Ratio is greater than one, that is a positive sign of liquidity, whereas a ratio less than one suggests a company that may be less liquid. The calculation for the Quick Ratio is:

$$\frac{\text{Cash} + \text{Trade Receivables (or equivalents)}}{\text{Total Current Liabilities}}$$

Sales/Receivables: Dividing a company's annual sales by the receivables stated on its balance sheet will calculate the number of times a company's receivables "turn over" in a given year, which is an indication of how fast a company's cash cycle is. For example, a company with annual sales of $1,000,000 and an accounts receivable balance of $250,000 turns its accounts receivable over four times per year. You should be careful, however, to make sure that you account for any seasonality in the business which would inflate the accounts receivable balance at a given point in time. Sales/Receivables is calculated as:

$$\frac{\text{Net Sales (Annual)}}{\text{Average Trade Receivables}}$$

Days' Receivable Outstanding: A corollary to Sales/Receivables is a calculation of the number of days of sales that are currently in accounts receivable, or put another way, the average number of days that receivables are outstanding. The higher this number, the greater the likelihood of collection risk with respect to the accounts receivable. Similarly, with Days' Receivable Outstanding, you must be careful to evaluate the level of accounts receivable at a specific period of time to make sure you have accounted for any seasonality. It is also helpful to evaluate the aging of the accounts receivable to understand any collection issues. The calculation for Days' Receivable Outstanding is:

$$\frac{365}{\text{Sales/Receivable Ratio}}$$

Cost of Sales/Inventory: Dividing a company's cost of sales by its inventory at a given time calculates the number of times inventory is turned over during the year. If this ratio is high, this suggests the company experiences greater liquidity with respect to its inventory or is better able to turn inventory into cash. Conversely, if this ratio is low, this suggests that the company's conversion cycle from inventory to cash is longer, or that the company has stale inventory that may not be readily convertible into cash. However, you must evaluate the reasons for a low turnover, as it might suggest that the company is building up material for some future sales event. Again, you must be careful when you are picking a point in time to calculate inventory to make sure you have accounted for any artificial increase or decrease in inventory at that point in time. You must also make sure that in your cost of sales calculation you are including only material costs and not service or labor costs. The calculation for Cost of Sales/Inventory is:

$$\frac{\text{Cost of Sales (Annual)}}{\text{Average Inventory}}$$

Days' Inventory Outstanding: Similar to the Days' Receivable Outstanding calculation, the Days' Inventory Outstanding calculation will yield the average length of time inventory items are on the balance sheet. The calculation for Days' Inventory Outstanding is:

$$\frac{365}{\text{Cost of Sales/Inventory Ratio}}$$

Cost of Sales/Payables: A company's Cost of Sales/Payables indicates how many times trade payables turn over during the year. A higher ratio suggests that the time between purchase and payment is short, whereas a lower ratio suggests a more extended period of time between purchase and payment, which can mean that the company is either experiencing cash flow challenges and is having problems paying vendors on time, the company is purposefully stretching its payables to increase the level of vendor financing, or that the company has issues with outstanding invoices. Similar to the Days' Inventory calculation issues, you must look at inventory levels over the course of the year to make sure the calculation is not skewed by seasonality.

$$\frac{\text{Cost of Sales}}{\text{Average Accounts Payable}}$$

Days' Payables Outstanding: The calculation of Days' Payables Outstanding, which measures the average length of time payables remain outstanding on the balance sheet. The calculation for Days' Payables Outstanding is:

$$\frac{365}{\text{Cost of Sales/Payable Ratio}}$$

In addition to the measures previously outlined, which focus on a company's liquidity or ability to pay its debts when they become due, buyers will also review a company's operating ratios to determine how effectively the business is managed, particularly in comparison to its industry.

Return on Equity: A company's Return on Equity (expressed as a percentage) measures the effectiveness of management in generating a return on the company's equity. While a high Return on Equity is generally a sign of effective management, it can also suggest an inadequately capitalized company (or a company with too much debt). Return on Equity is calculated as:

$$\frac{\text{Net Income}}{\text{Stockholders' Equity}}$$

Multiply result by 100%

Return on Assets: A company's Return on Assets (also expressed as a percentage) measures the effectiveness of management in generating a return on the company's overall assets. While a high Return on Assets is generally a sign of effective management, it can also suggest an inadequately capitalized company (or a company with too few or heavily depreciated assets). When reviewing a company's Return on Assets, you will also want to understand what assets the company is leasing and include the capitalized cost of these assets to help develop a more complete picture. Return on Assets is calculated as:

$$\frac{\text{Net Income}}{\text{Net Assets}}$$

Multiply result by 100%

LaVergne, TN USA
04 June 2010
185062LV00002B/2/P